Bloom Where

Transformational Strategies Empowering You To Grow Through
What You Go Through

Ronetta J. Francis, JD

Bloom Where You Are Planted

Contents

Bloom Where You Are Planted

DEDICATION

This book is dedicated to my grandmother, Carrie E. Byrd.

She was an enterprising, serial entrepreneur – a Jane of All Trades.

There wasn't anything she could not do – nor any subject she didn't know *something* about.

She knew everybody and was always happy to help anyone in need.

She was proud of her family and loved us fiercely – always challenging us to be our very best.

I love you and I miss you.

I hope to continue to make you proud.

Bloom Where You Are Planted

ACKNOWLEDGEMENTS

Thank you to my Lord and Savior for the gift of this anointed life, now and everlasting; for your Divine Love, and Grace. You are my Provider and the Source from which all blessings flow.

Thank you to my dearest family and friends who have supported and encouraged me every step of the way, not only in the process of writing this book, but in every aspect of my life – especially to my beloved husband, Earl C. Francis, Jr., and daughters, Jordan, Dana and Erica; my mother, Joyce W. Green; my sister, Tanya A. Burke; and my brother, Kevin W. Green – I am because of you.

To my Sister Circle, who lift me up and hold me down – Evelyn, Roz, Elecia, Celia, Kimberly, Liz, Kathy, Cole, Alison, Dionne, Aleachia, my sisters of Alpha Kappa Alpha Sorority, Inc., and friends of The Links, Incorporated – and a special shout-out to the OGs at the University of Alabama: Shanta, Armeter, Sylvia, April, Danae and Anita – I say, "Roll Tide!"

To my mentors, coaches and sponsors – particularly Cora, Esther, Phyllis, Claire, Ryane, and Toby – thank you see my spark and investing in its potential.

To Suzanne Anderson, whose sage advice set me on a path that forever changed my life; and to to Pastor Carruthers, for laying out the battle plan.

To Robin Kelley, for your Eagle Eye.

To Johnny Mack – GPS: Get Published Successfully, for your consultation and guidance.

There are so many others to thank and I wish I could include everyone by name. Please know that I truly appreciate your love and support, and that your name is written with deep gratitude in my heart.

Bloom Where You Are Planted

PREFACE

Bloom Where You Are Planted. The concepts and principles behind this philosophy have been a part of my life for the better part of 20 years. I have shared the ***Bloom Where You Are Planted*** message with countless attendees at various professional and leadership conferences; it even served as the foundation for several executive leadership mentoring groups that I led during my tenure as a corporate officer in Ethics and Compliance for the Fortune One company. My now-adult children were raised with this phrase reverberating in their heads, and hopefully in their hearts. With such deep familiarity with the material, I had sporadically entertained the idea that I should write a book and share the inspiring message that the ***Bloom Where You Are Planted*** philosophy offers with a wider audience. Yet, when it came to me actually writing the book, there were many delays, starts and stops, and many other barriers, real and perceived, that got in the way.

My Inner Critic screamed, "Who are you? What makes what you have to say so important? What makes you think you are in a position to share anything? Who do you think is going to listen?" And I tell you, my Inner Critic was loud and convincing. She spoke these self-limiting, fear-based beliefs into existence, and I allowed it. I allowed these thoughts to take root and grow. And even though I knew the benefit and impact of sharing such a positive message – that it had the capacity to provide a sense of inspiration and empowerment – it wasn't rocket science or some earth-shattering, groundbreaking discovery. So, believing my Inner Critic, I put the drafts of a manuscript back in the file cabinet and closed the door.

Then, life happened. And I found myself facing a rather challenging and unexpected storm. Trying to navigate my way through this rough storm, I struggled to make sense of what was happening to me. I did not see a path forward – I could not figure out how I was going to make it through. I was defeated.

And so it was, that in the midst of this storm, during a particularly emotional period, my husband walked into our bedroom and saw my despair. Doing what he does best, which is to make me laugh, he said, "I'm sorry, babe, that you are going through this. I wish there were a way I could help. Wouldn't it be nice if there were a book or something that could, you know, teach you how to bloom where you are planted?" Smiling through my tears, I responded, "Yes, it really would."
Yep, I think I'll keep him. 🙂

Ronetta

INTRODUCTION

What does it mean to Bloom Where You Are Planted?

The phrase is not new and has been interpreted to mean that one should make the most of what they have and play the cards that have been dealt; to pull oneself up by their bootstraps; to basically "Suck it up, buttercup." While the phrase can certainly have these connotations, the fundamental sentiment is consistent and has not changed. Though I didn't realize it at the time, the seeds for the Bloom Where You Are Planted philosophy of transformational change – the seeds of Faith, Positive Attitude, Gratitude, and Hard Work had been deeply embedded within my core value system at an early age. These were the core values that I would turn to time and time again – whenever faced with a challenge, life decision, etc.

There is a common belief that if one is dissatisfied with some aspect of their life, they should **do** something about it; that if you just do something different, then a different result will surely follow. Yet, in order to bring about authentic change, one must go through an internal transformation: the seeds for greater growth and development must be planted and nurtured, changing the essence of our **being** – our beliefs, our thoughts – before we can **have** our full bloom. Growth requires change. Nothing can grow unchanged. You cannot go through an experience great or small, wonderful or unpleasant, and remain the same. Each experience molds and shapes us. What shape we take on, how we evolve as we go through each experience, is up to us.

xi

Bloom Where You Are Planted

We may not always be able to control the experiences we may face. In those circumstances, rather than looking for ways to change our experiences or our environment, the challenge – and the basis of authentic transformational change – is to change our perspective on those experiences, assess and take ownership of how we are contributing to the experience and to release those negative influences (internal and external) that no longer serve us, thereby allowing us to learn and grow from each experience.

In essence, to Bloom Where You Are Planted is to grow through what you go through

Chapter 1: PREPARE YOUR SOUL
Faith

With faith no larger than a mustard seed, you can tell the mountain to move from here to there. And it would. Everything would be possible for you. – Matthew 17: 20-21

THERE ARE NO COINCIDENCES

A peculiar thing happened as I began writing this chapter. The original title was simply, "Prepare Your Soil," to align with the gardening analogies for the "Bloom Where You Are Planted" theme. However, each time I typed this title, "Prepare Your Soul" kept popping up in its place. The first time this happened, I chuckled to myself and thought, "Hmm. Isn't that ironic? What a coincidence – this chapter is about faith and I typed 'soul' instead of 'soil!'" Well, after deleting that "error" and typing the title again – I did the same thing.

So, after the third time making the same "typo," it dawned on me that I do not actually believe in coincidences; things happen for a reason. I say it all the time: "There are no coincidences, just Divine Providence." For me, this means that events come to pass and our lives cross paths with others at a particular time for a reason – all as a part of God's Divine Plan. We may not always recognize or appreciate the meaning or the significance of the event, or the encounter, or the relationship while it is happening (or even after it has already happened) – yet, nonetheless, it is – I believe – all part of His Plan.

With this firmly held belief of Divine Providence, I really try hard to pay attention – to be alert and present in the moment – when I bump into someone "by accident." What did we discuss? Why did our paths cross? What was I supposed to share or gain from the encounter? Was there an additional connection or introduction to be made for the benefit of someone else? (You know, like when you run into Bobbie, who works for XYZ Corporation, and she tells you she has just been promoted and is searching for a new administrative assistant. And then you remember your conversation last week with Danny, who was an amazing administrative assistant when you both worked together at Acme, Inc. two years ago, and who happens to be searching for a new role because he was laid off after a corporate merger?)

All of these questions race through my mind as I try to process – in real-time – the meaning or significance of a "chance encounter." And I engage in these introspective exercises for a reason. Life has taught me not

2

to take these experiences for granted. There have been far too many "Aha" moments for me to ignore: moments where I have connected the dots; moments where I appreciated the perfect timing of running into an old acquaintance; or moments where hearing an otherwise extraneous or incidental word or phrase was just the message I needed to hear at that time.

So, taking my hands off the keyboard, I relented. At that moment, I accepted the truth that this first chapter, which serves as the true foundation for exploring how to Bloom Where You Are Planted, does, in fact, require preparation of one's soul. Such preparation is essential to embrace the faith-based principles – the root system – through which growth and development occur. Without which, we are just surviving, not thriving, and unable to achieve our desired full bloom.

Walk By Faith – Not By Sight

UNCHARTED WATERS

This journey of self-exploration, growth, and development, of being able to seek and realize a positive benefit from any situation or set of circumstances, to bloom where you are planted, is firmly rooted in one's faith.

Now, believe me: I am well aware that bringing up the discussion of one's faith can have a myriad of outcomes. I have long been schooled by my elders and mentors that it is a best practice to avoid discussing topics dealing with either politics or religion in the workplace and, quite frankly, in most social settings.

And I have, in the past, studiously followed this advice. Doing so afforded me the ability to steer clear of any issues that may run near and dear to a particular individual; the dexterity to tread lightly near those issues that define a person's identity and character (what makes that person who they are and what they believe); and the capacity to exercise extreme caution around those issues that can either forge indestructible bonds or obliterate any ties or connections.

In reality, these are the issues that either create allies or foes. And, let's be honest, those who are very astute at navigating the unwritten and unspoken political minefields within any organization would agree with the premise that one needs to be mindful (dare I say, intentional) when either creating an alliance or an adversarial relationship. It is important to be aware of the potential outcomes since the formation of such a relationship could be either a career-defining success or a career-limiting failure.

However, treading the waters of political correctness will only sustain you for a period of time. At some pivotal moment, and you will know it when the time comes, one must be bold enough to take a stand on those issues that are truly important to them, trusting and believing that

4

those who are intended to align with that stance will do so. For me, this is such a moment.

In order for us to connect, for there to be a meeting of the minds and hearts in sharing this message, I believe it's necessary to be as transparent and authentic as I possibly can. And for me to do that requires that I share with you, quite simply, that my faith as a Christian serves as the foundation for all that I am, for all that I do, and for all that I hope to become.

But, before I continue, I must offer this confession: while my faith is central to who I am as an individual – a Black woman, daughter, sister, wife, mother, friend, attorney, author, speaker, and coach – I am not a learned biblical scholar. Rather, I am an avid learner of the Bible and its teachings. I consider it a lifelong learning process – every day there are new lessons to learn and new wonders to behold.

To be honest (again with more honesty: when will this confession end?), in my youth, as a result of years of Sunday School, summer Vacation Bible School, and countless Easter and Christmas speeches, I could tell you, from memory and without hesitation, the books of the Bible – in order. Today, however, in the age of electronics and technology, without shame I tell you that I rely (heavily) on the Bible app to get me to the book and verse I'm studying or reading.

I think it's important to acknowledge that one can possess a deep faith without being an accomplished biblical scholar. While not having a deep knowledge of all the books of the Bible, or being able to quote chapter and verse at will, might be a barrier to some folks actually talking about their faith and learning more – Bloom Where You Are Planted is firmly rooted in going over, around and breaking through barriers.

I have often said, "But I not only know who I am, but I know *whose* I am." That refinement of self-identity has been especially important as I have gone through life's challenges and triumphs, peaks and valleys: from job successes and advancements to career setbacks and disappointments; from winning and losing federal trials; from the joys and pains of experiencing motherhood with successful pregnancies (twice) and the utter devastation and isolating heartbreak with pregnancy losses through miscarriages (also twice); from running an emotional marathon with my partner in life and love (married 25 years – and counting). Through it all, I continue to hold fast to the belief that God is the Source of and for my life – with all of its blessings and misfortunes.

As my Source, God is the provider of all the resources to supply my needs, whether those needs are love, acceptance, companionship, provisions for health, safety and shelter, or sources of income. My goal is not to rely on or put my faith in any of these resources – people, places or things – because each one is transitory; temporary. They can be depleted or taken away at a moment's notice. However, with my reliance on and faith in God, who is eternal, as my Source, then He has the power, agency, and ability to replace, renew or restore whatever resource has been moved, changed or depleted.

Even with these firmly held beliefs, I do not hold the view that my faith in God will prevent unfortunate, even catastrophic events from occurring in the world, negatively impacting me, my family, friends, and others around me. Quite the contrary. I am fully aware that, in this journey called life, storms will come – but so will the rainbows; heartbreak and pain are a given – but so is laughter and love; want and need, along with abundant overflow.

With these myriad ebbs and flows of life, I certainly do not hold all the answers, but my faith gives me a resting place – a refuge in the middle of the storm, peace and comfort during pain, and a confidence that all my needs will be supplied. I can truly rest in the knowledge that there is a Higher Purpose, a Higher Calling, to this earthly experience.

My intention in sharing this information is not an attempt to proselytize or to exclude anyone of a different faith (or nonbelievers), but merely to share with you what has helped me Grow Through What I Have Gone Through in the hopes that it may enlighten, strengthen, reinforce or facilitate your journey as you Bloom Where You Are Planted.

FAITH
is not believing that God can . . .
it is knowing that God will.

UNDIVIDED ATTENTION

The morning of June 13, 2017 began just like countless other Tuesday mornings; nothing really remarkable or outside of my normal routine. I do recall, though, as I drove into work that day, appreciating the beautiful weather we were experiencing in northwest Arkansas. The sky was clear and bright and the temperature was in the low 80s – a perfectly picturesque spring morning.

As the Vice President for U.S. Ethics and Compliance for the Fortune 1 company, I had a rather busy agenda for the day, including various meetings, conference calls, numerous project status briefings, and a couple of Mentor-Mentee meetings – a typical workday. Kicking it all off though, was a routine one-on-one meeting with my boss. While I waited outside her office for her current meeting to end and ours to begin, I reviewed the latest U.S. Ethics' department metrics and significant internal investigative case developments, glanced at my notes detailing the progress being made toward specific team and corporate objectives, and chatted casually with other members of the team as they walked by.

When it was time for our meeting, my boss opened her office door and invited me in – even though the attendee from her previous meeting, our department's HR representative, was still in the room. Not an uncommon or unusual occurrence. With so many corporate meetings scheduled back-to-back, and usually without a time buffer in between, there is frequent participant overlap – which can take on the look and feel of a relay race, with one meeting attendee passing the baton to the next

8

one in line. However, when the HR representative did not excuse himself from the room and merely repositioned his seating around the conference table, I knew immediately that this meeting with my boss was not going to be the one-on-one update I had anticipated.

The obligatory morning greetings were exchanged, followed by the banal question: "How are you, Ronetta?" Ordinarily, a question inquiring about your well-being is positively received and appreciated. However, reading the tone and body language of the two meeting participants, my intuition was screaming, "Something's not right!!" I was instantly on high alert. Curious and suspicious, the only response I could muster was a controlled: "I don't know – how AM I?"

The discussion that followed literally caused a shift in my personal space-time continuum; my world had been rocked, as they say. Not only rocked, but everything I previously understood about my world, and my place in it, began to erode – breaking apart bit by bit – and breaking me along with it. During that discussion, my employer essentially informed me that my services to the organization were no longer valued or needed. While the foundation of the discussion was grounded in such nonjudgmental terms as "organizational realignment" and "role consolidation," and topped off with assurances that this outcome was not the result of any personal or professional failures or deficiencies on my part, the end result was simple. And even though it took me years to admit it to myself, or to say the words out loud – the fact remained: I was fired.

Bloom Where You Are Planted

Let me tell you, as an employment attorney for more than 25 years and a corporate executive in ethics and compliance, I know a thing or two about employment terminations. I have investigated and challenged the legality of some terminations in federal court; I have counseled corporate clients on how to structure, communicate and implement widespread layoffs; I have even had to deliver termination decisions myself.

And, even in today's economy, with the ever-growing frequency of employee terminations resulting from business closures, staff reductions, mergers and acquisitions, leadership changes and so on, I must confess that neither the commonness of its existence nor my professional expertise prepared me for, or protected me against, the avalanche of widespread emotions that would overtake me in the days, weeks and months to come.

But upon leaving that office and returning to the bright and beautiful Tuesday morning still waiting outside, I could not help but to stop, mid-stride in the parking lot on the way back to my car, and laugh. (I told y'all my space-time continuum had shifted, right?) I laughed, not because I was losing my mind, or had just heard a funny joke, or had seen a montage of my favorite movie bloopers.

I laughed because I became aware, in that instance, that when God desires a certain outcome – it's going to happen. The simple truth was that, for nearly 18 months before this beautiful, sunny Tuesday morning, I knew deep in my soul that it was time to move on in my career – to a new team, or a new division, or to a new company; whatever the new venture was really didn't matter because it was time to move on.

10

I ignored and downplayed the signs, warnings and conversations I had with my friends and mentors outright telling me that this position I was in was no longer good for me. Not that I couldn't do the work – and do it well – but that the organization and its leadership changes were not good for me, personally, or for my professional career.

Yet, for a multitude of reasons, including fear, pride, and stubbornness, I ignored the signs. After all, I was an educated professional, accustomed to being "the first" or "the only" and well acquainted with working hard to achieve my goals. It was inconceivable to me that work ethic, results, personality, and organizational equity would not prevail – I was not going to be run off from a job that I had worked so hard to earn.

But, after 18 months of me ignoring and downplaying the signs and warnings, which were really God's Whispers tapping me on my shoulder and calling me to follow His Plan, enough was enough. It was time for me to go – and now, there was no way for me to dispute or get around that fact. So, there I stood in the middle of the corporate parking lot, laughing, and pointing to the sky, saying: "Yes, God!! Now you have my undivided attention – I am listening."

A TEST OF FAITH

The afternoon of June 13, 2017, I kicked into auto-pilot mode, and the goal-driven, detail-oriented, determined strategist took over. My mission was clear: I had to find another job. And as the primary wage-earner for my family, with one recent college graduate and another with three years remaining in her college career, I needed to find a new job immediately.

Now, even though I had not actively searched for employment in more than 20 years, and a lot had changed, I knew enough of the basics to get started. So, I jumped in and embraced my new reality: from that day on, looking for a full-time job would be my full-time job.

And I worked hard at my job. I spent the next two years leveraging my vast network of personal and professional connections, emailing, calling, texting for leads, introductions or referrals – basically doing anything I could to aid in my active search for employment, including resume building and rebuilding; updating social media profiles; applying for jobs after recruiters raved over the depth, quality, and scope of my professional experiences; and, investing thousands of dollars in continuing education, personal and leadership development seminars, workshops and programs. And all without a single job offer to show for it.

How is that possible? How can a seasoned legal and business professional, known for being a strategic, solutions-oriented, trusted, well-regarded leader with strong executive presence and outstanding

12

communication skills, who followed all of the professional advice on "What to do when you get fired" and "How to bounce back after you get fired," not have a single job offer to entertain in nearly two years? Let me tell you that it is possible – because that is exactly what happened. And because it happened, the embarrassment, shame, pain, humiliation, self-doubt, depression, and anger I experienced as a result of being fired was amplified – exponentially – by this two-year period of consistent rejection.

I had no doubt that I was being tested – and so was my faith. How could I hold my head up and face another day, when all I wanted to do was shrink away and disappear? How could I leave my house, smile and be pleasant to others when all I wanted to do was yell and scream? How could I be a light for my family, when all I saw was darkness? I was truly being tested – and I felt like I was failing miserably!

Faith. It does not make things easy; it makes them possible.

GOD'S PERFECT TIMING

On August 26, 2018, in support of my sorority's (Alpha Kappa Alpha Sorority, Inc.) International Day of Prayer, I attended worship service with 30 of my sorority sisters at The Dwelling Place in Fayetteville, Arkansas. At this point, I was more than one year into my job search and I was feeling defeated. During that service, Pastor Marcus Carruthers delivered a message, "Prepare For Battle," which I am convinced, was ordained, anointed, inspired and written just for me!

His message reminded me that while seasons may change, God will always remain the same. He emphasized that there is nothing we go through that is too difficult for God to fix; He can take a mistake and turn it into a miracle. I was blessed with the assurance that God is sufficient – He will always be enough. And that despite the challenges I was going through and the weight of the burden that felt unbearable, my breakthrough was on the way; my victory was on the way!

That glorious and triumphant message of God's Power and His Promise directed my prayers and meditations and inspired me to sketch out a sort of roadmap of the faith-based principles that had equipped me to face my challenging struggles from a position of power and victory, rather than from uncertainty and defeat.

Bloom Where You Are Planted

My Combat Survival Guide

- ***Be Faithful – Obey God's Word***
    - *And without faith, it is impossible to please Him, for he who comes to God must believe that He is and that He is a rewarder of those who seek Him.* Hebrews 11:6 NASB
    - *And my God will meet all your needs according to the riches of his glory in Christ Jesus.* Philippians 4:19 NIV
    - Obedience to God's Word is the key to His Blessings
    - We must expect God to do what He says He will do
    - If we are faithful to use what we have today, in obedience to God's Word, God will help us to face the battle and to overcome any obstacles
    - It is an Act of Faith to step out – to do the scary – to do the unknown – to do the unthinkable

- ***Praise God at All Times – In Times of Celebration and In Times of Struggle***
    - *Rejoice in the Lord always. I will say it again: Rejoice! Let your gentleness be evident to all. The Lord is near. Do not be anxious about anything, but in every situation, by prayer and petition, with thanksgiving, present your requests to God. And the peace of God, which transcends all understanding, will guard your hearts and your minds in Christ Jesus.* Philippians 4:4-7 NIV
    - *I will extol the Lord at all times; his praise will always be on my lips.* Psalm 34:1 NIV
    - *Consider it pure joy whenever you face trials because you know that the testing of your faith produces perseverance, which leads to a mature and finished work that is lacking in nothing.* James 1:2 NIV

15

o God is waiting on us to trust Him through whatever test or battle we are facing. He uses the challenging situations to strengthen us. When going through a battle – we must trust and praise Him because He is working on our behalf.

- ***Persevere Through the Test***

   o *Learn to be patient, so you will please God and be given what He has promised.* Hebrews 10:36 CEV

   o *Cast your cares on the Lord and He will sustain you; He will never let the righteous be shaken.* Psalm 55:22 NIV

   o For perspective, do not focus on the challenge, rather keep your eyes and your heart focused on God, as the Source that sustains us.

   o God's Blessings will be revealed; so, do not become weary; continue to keep the faith. Know that God is sufficient.

- ***Do the Work***

   o *Commit to the Lord whatever you do, and He will establish your plans.* Proverbs 16:3 NIV

   o *But seek first his kingdom and his righteousness, and all these things will be given to you as well. Therefore, do not worry about tomorrow, for tomorrow will worry about itself. Each day has enough trouble of its own.* Matthew 6:33-34

   o *Show your faith through your deeds and actions; for faith without deeds is useless.* James 2:17-20 NIV

   o When you put the work that God has called you to do first, then all your needs for food, clothing, or shelter will be provided.

   o During your challenge, God is working out those things that need to be addressed. Do not panic. Do not be shaken by doubt or by not knowing how/when/why to take action.

- **Prepare For His Promises**
  - *For I know the plans that I have for you declares the Lord, plans for welfare and not for Calamity to give you a future and a hope. Then you will call upon me and come and pray to me and I will listen to you. You will seek Me and find Me when you search for Me with all your heart.* Jeremiah 29:11-13 NASB
  - *A man's gift maketh room for him and bringeth him before great men.* Proverbs 18:16 ASV
  - *Blessed is the one who perseveres under trial because, having stood the test, that person will receive the crown of life that the Lord has promised to those who love Him.* James 1:12 NIV

I have certainly grown through the consistent use of My Combat Survival Guide, and I continue to add to it and refine it to ensure that it really speaks to me and my needs. That message and this Guide were exactly what I needed to lift my spirits, to encourage me and to strengthen my resolve as I continued my job search – and my quest for God's Plan for my life.

CONFIRMATION OF GOD'S PLAN

After such a powerful message on Preparing for Battle, I ventured back to The Dwelling Place the following week to see what other insights I might be able to discover. I was curious to know how I might be able to grow during this season; what tasks might I be called to complete in accordance with God's Plan? So, even though a different leader delivered

17

the message, the impact on me was just as striking. He entitled this message, also anointed and ordained and written specifically for me, "I'm Still Here."

In this message, the minister shared that, despite our many trials and tribulations, all of these experiences are preparing me – setting me up – for what God has planned for me. He explained the necessity of having to go through the valleys in order to appreciate the peaks; that the lows are just as critical as the highs.

But what the minister said next was what literally blew me away: he began an analogy that expounded on the uncomfortable and sometimes challenging experiences one must endure before realizing the abundant blessings of the season that closely mirrored the concepts, ideals, and principles that I had outlined in the first draft of the Bloom Where You Are Planted manuscript.

Specifically, when it preached that in order to enjoy the harvest, the seed must be prepared and planted; that there is a process the seed must go through to get rooted to become closer to God; and that once the seed is firmly rooted, no matter what elements it may be exposed to (such as wind and rain, which the minister equated to the loss of a job/house/income), during the rest of its growth and development, the seed is still covered.

I was so touched by this message that, even after the service concluded, it took me a few moments to gather my composure and dry my tears before I could stand to leave. I was overwhelmingly engulfed in the power of the message. I am so thankful for God's covering over my life. I know, without a shadow of a doubt, that in the midst of it all, God still had me covered and that I had no need to worry. He would handle it. It also became very clear to me, the exact confirmation I had been seeking, that as part of God's Plan, the message I had been working on for this book was something that I needed to complete and to share.

DO IT AFRAID

As I look back over the two-year period since that bright and beautiful Tuesday morning, I find it ironic that in the midst of my darkest hours and times of despair, I also accomplished some amazing things, both personally and professionally. I met and collaborated with some of the nation's most dynamic and inspirational leaders; I attended several professional networking and development conferences, spoke in front of thousands of professional women, and worked with a lifestyle coach to rediscover my brilliance, while learning to put "fear" in its place and stand confidently in my own power.

I also co-authored an Amazon.com best-selling book, *"Champions Never Tell: Sisters Surviving Storms in the Workplace,"* and began working on my first solo writing project, *"Bloom Where You Are Planted."* I also rebranded myself and upgraded my skills and experiences and started my own consulting firm to focus on executive coaching and leadership development. I experienced joy, satisfaction, self-confidence, a sense of pride and achievement, and renewed self-esteem. Life is strange and wonderful like that: it is never all one thing or another.

So, after much prayer and overwhelming confirmation, I stepped out on faith. I walked away from the fear that kept me knocking on closed doors in the corporate world – because that was the world I knew well and where I was most comfortable – and moved toward the promise of walking in my purpose, of being uncomfortable as I continue to grow along this journey of sharing my story in the hopes of empowering, inspiring and uplifting others along the way.

Even though I am stepping out on faith and away from fear, I am afraid. But I know now what I must do: I must do it afraid.

Feed your faith and your fear will starve.

SOUL SUPPORT

When I think about embarking upon a journey or starting a new project or adventure or just going through my day, I need a roadmap – or a guide – of some sort. Whether it is actual turn-by-turn directions from Google Maps, or a detailed project plan, or my trusted calendar and planner, these tools and resources help ensure that my guided endeavors will successfully lead me to my desired destination. Case in point: My Combat Soul

Survival Guide provided me with encouragement and support for my good days, and most importantly, for my challenging days. It provided a guiding light through one of my darkest periods and fiercest battles, and it continues to do so today.

Likewise, as you embark upon this journey to Bloom Where You Are Planted, I invite you to use the Guide. Customize and tailor it to your specific needs so that it provides you with the support you will need for this experience. However, whether or not you use the Guide or any modification thereof, is really not the critical point. The takeway is that you should have an instrument of some type that is a source of encouragement and support; some behavior or activity that touches and enriches your soul; or some channel through which your spirit is renewed and your focus is clarified.

For this life-changing journey, ask yourself: What will I do to prepare my mind, body and soul – not just for this transformational development process, but for any of life's challenges that lie ahead? What resources do I have to call upon? How will I know when my natural resources (emotional, physical and spiritual) are being depleted? And what will/can I do to restore these resources? What do I have in my life that I can turn to for strength, guidance and support?

I encourage each of you, regardless of where you are on your faith journey, to incorporate the following activities in your daily life. These soul-supporting activities will also help to strengthen your body and ease your mind, and will provide you with a strong framework, successfully leading you to your desired destination.

- Be Thankful – Actively practice gratitude by thanking someone daily
- Be Helpful – Provide loving assistance to someone in need
- Smile Often – Laugh daily; do something fun that makes you smile
- Be Adventurous – Try something new; do something "for the first time"
- Be Generous – Give of your time and talents for the benefit of someone else
- Socialize – Spend time building relationships with other people
- Go outside – Disconnect from technology; connect with nature
- Meditate – Be mindful of your presence; practice being "in the moment"
- Journal – Keep a record of your journey; honor your emotions and experiences
- Exercise – Find a routine that works for you; just keep moving
- Eat Well – Make healthy food choices; practice portion control
- Rest – Eliminate nightly stressors; clear your mind to renew your body
- Pray – Spend time deepening your personal relationship with your source of Higher Power: God, the Father, Jehovah, Allah, Waheguru, Jah, Vishnu, Mother Earth, the Creator, the Universe, the Divine

FAITH

I can do the impossible

I can see the invisible

Because I got faith

I can climb a mountain

I can reach my goal

More than a conqueror

Down in my soul

Devil is a liar

I've won the race

Said I got victory

All because I got faith. YEAH

-by God's Property, Kirk Franklin

DIGGING DEEPER
PREPARING YOUR SOUL – FAITH

 My mother once shared with me a document called God's Yellow Pages. I have referred to it often and passed it on to countless others. If you aren't already familiar with it, I have included a portion of the references below, as an introduction. If you would like to see more, you can find the complete guide at http://dalesdesigns.net/yellow_pages.htm

WHEN FEELING:		
Afraid	**Faith Fails**	**Protected**
Psalm 34:4	Psalm 42:5	Psalm 18:1-3
Matthew 10:28	Hebrews 11	Psalm 34:7
2 Timothy 1:7	**Friends Fail**	**Sick - In Pain**
Hebrews 13:5,6	Psalm 41:9-13	Psalm 38
Anxious	Luke 17:3,4	Matthew 26:39
Psalm 46	Romans 12:14,17,19,21	Romans 5:3-5
Matthew 6:19-34	2 Timothy 4:16-18	2 Corinthians 12:9,10

Bloom Where You Are Planted

	WHEN FEELING:	
Philippians 4:6	**Leaving Home**	1 Peter 4:12,13,19
1 Peter 5:6,7	Psalm 121	**Sorrowful**
Backsliding	Matthew 10:16-20	Psalm 51
Psalm 51	**Lonely**	Matthew 5:4
1 John 1:4-9	Psalm 23	John 14
Bereaved	Hebrews 13:5,6	2 Corinthians 1:3,4
Matthew 5:4	**Needing God's Protection**	1 Thessalonians 4:13-18
2 Corinthians 1:3,4	Psalm 27:1-3	**Tempted**
Bitter - Critical	Psalm 91	Psalm 1
1 Corinthians 13	Philippians 4:19	Psalm 139:23,24
Conscious of Sin	**Needing Guidance**	Matthew 26:41
Proverbs 28:13	Psalm 32:8	1 Corinthians 10:12-14
Defeated	Proverbs 3:5,6	Philippians 4:8
Romans 8:31-39	**Needing Peace**	James 4:7

WHEN FEELING:

Depressed	John 14:1-4	2 Peter 2:9,3:17
Psalm 34	John 16:33	**Thankful**
Disaster Threatens	Romans 5:1-5	Psalm 100
Psalm 91	Philippians 4:6,7	1 Thessalonians 5:18
Psalm 118:5,6	**Needing Rules For Life**	Hebrews 13:15
Luke 8:22-25	Romans 12	
Discouraged	**Overcome**	**Traveling**
Psalm 23	Psalm 6	Psalm 121
Psalm 42:6-11	Romans 8:31-39	**In Trouble**
Psalm 55:22	1 John 1:4-9	Psalm 16+31
Matthew 5:11,12	**Prayerful**	John 14:1-4
2 Corinthians 4:8-18	Psalm 4	Hebrews 7:25
Philippians 4:4-7	Psalm 42	**Weary**
Doubting	Luke 11:1-13	Psalm 90

Bloom Where You Are Planted

WHEN FEELING:		
Matthew 8:26	John 17	Matthew 11:28-30
Hebrews 11	1 John 5:14,15	1 Corinthians 15:58
Facing Crisis		Galatians 6:9,10
Psalm 121		**Worried**
Matthew 6:25-34		Matthew 6:19-34
Hebrews 11		1 Peter 5:6,7

Chapter 2: PREPARE YOUR SEEDS/CHOOSE YOUR TOOLS
Set the Stage for Transformational Change

You don't need a new year or a new date to start over. You only need a new mindset.

"BLOOM WHERE YOU ARE PLANTED" – ITS HISTORICAL ORIGIN AND USAGE

While many people believe the phrase, "Bloom Where You Are Planted" originates from the Bible, I could not find any evidence to support that belief. And trust me, I did my research. What I did find were a few passages that could be stretched to somewhat align with the tone and spirit of the message behind the phrase. For example, Psalms 92:13 mentions that when good people take root in God's House, they will flourish. And Jeremiah 17:7-8 equates a person who puts their trust and confidence in God to a tree that is planted near water – a tree that does not fear heat or drought, its leaves are always green, and it continually bears fruit. There are other references, but none that are directly on point.

My research also revealed that Saint Francis de Sales (1567-1622), the Bishop of Geneva, has been credited with coining the phrase, "Bloom Where You Are Planted." His actual quote, however, was the following: "Truly charity has no limit; for the love of God has been poured into our hearts by His Spirit dwelling in each one of us, calling us to a life of devotion and inviting us to bloom in the garden He has planted and directing us to radiate the beauty and spread the fragrance of His Providence."

Mary Engelbreit, a graphic artist and children's book illustrator, popularized the phrase in today's modern culture when she included it in many of her illustrations in the 1980s.

A flower does not think of competing with the flower next to it –

it just

BLOOMS

Today, various iterations of her illustrations have been commercialized

and transformed into images, such as the one here, gracing posters, photo album covers, calendars and even iron-on transfers for t-shirts.

In fact, if you venture into any crafts or home decor store, you are likely to discover a print, framed embroidery, wooden plaque or canvas, emblazoned with the inspirational message to Bloom. And as you can probably visualize – yes, my home office proudly showcases at least four pieces of floral art, reminding me daily to live my best life.

MY INTRODUCTION TO BLOOM WHERE YOU ARE PLANTED

Even though the phrase, "Bloom Where You Are Planted" has been a part of our collective conversation for at least 500 years, the first time I heard it was March 2000. I was a trial attorney with the Dallas District Office of the U.S. Equal Employment Opportunity Commission (EEOC), assigned as the lead litigator for my very first federal employment discrimination case. I was representing a Spanish-speaking woman who alleged that she was unlawfully denied job assignments by her employer, a temporary staffing company, because she was pregnant. I was a brand-new trial attorney, having only been at the EEOC for about 18 months. Needless to say, I was more than a little anxious – did I mention that I had *never* tried a case, let alone before a federal judge and jury? And I wanted everything to go well.

In my capacity as a trial attorney with the EEOC, I represented individuals in single-party and class-action lawsuits on their claims of unlawful discrimination in the workplace. I knew the pain and hurt that they had experienced both as a result of the alleged unlawful actions of their employers and as a result of their decision to actually pursue their remedies in court: to file a lawsuit and endure the long, drawn-out and tedious process of litigation. Depending on the judge's caseload, scheduling considerations and other factors, it could easily take more than a year for a case to proceed through the litigation process and eventually make its way to trial. The emotional toll borne by our clients was never

32

lost on me and I took it as a personal mission to always do my very best, and to advocate at the highest level on each client's behalf.

Well, after I was assigned the case, it didn't take long for me to discover that the opposing attorney, representing the temporary staffing company, fit nearly every negative stereotype generally ascribed to legal professionals. Of course, I had heard all the snarky jokes about lawyers not being very honest and forthright – even being downright sneaky. Well, this guy was all of that – and more. He was conniving, rude, unprofessional and uncooperative at every turn; he took the adversarial process to a level I never anticipated or expected – nor was I prepared for.

Now, I understood that we were on opposite sides of the issues being litigated – and that we were both charged to zealously represent our respective clients – but what I couldn't quite understand was why he had to be so contentious and rude. Why did he find it necessary to treat me with such contempt and disrespect? Did he act this way with all opposing counsel – or was I special for some reason? Could he sense my trial inexperience and, like a shark feverishly tracking the scent of blood, be determined to hunt and destroy me? Being new to this area of practicing law, I found it quite a challenge to navigate this professional relationship and do the best job I could do for my clients. I really wanted to tell that guy to shove it where the sun doesn't shine, but I couldn't stoop that low. I had to maintain my professional integrity.

Bloom Where You Are Planted

And so, there I stood, at my dream job, fulfilling my life's mission, advocating and fighting for the elimination of discrimination in the workplace – doing what I love – only to realize that it was a hard, hard struggle.

I no longer had the answers; I needed help. I needed support, guidance, directions; maybe some legal strategies and tactics to stop this guy in his tracks and make him think twice about how he was dealing with me. So, in the middle of trial preparation, I went to my supervising trial attorney, Suzanne Anderson, and laid out my complaints, issues and concerns about the case and the difficulty I was experiencing with opposing counsel. Being the smart-as-a-whip, funny and fierce, straight-shooting Texas lawyer that Suzanne was (and continues to be), she just looked at me and said, "Well, Ronetta, you've just got to bloom where you're planted." Then, she turned and walked away. That was it.

I had to sit there and think about what she said – because this was the very first time I had ever heard that phrase. Truthfully, I wasn't quite sure what it meant. The first thing that came to mind was basically: Suck it up, buttercup. You may not like the cards you've been dealt, but just play the best hand you can and learn to roll with the punches. Make the most of it. And that's what I did. I sucked it up. I ignored the rudeness and held him accountable for his lack of cooperation and professionalism, and I worked tirelessly to prepare for trial. I researched all the legal issues and ensured all the witnesses were prepared for their testimony. I rehearsed my opening remarks and closing statements. I was ready with my "Objection, Your Honor!" (Yes, I practiced that, too!) I knew every angle of the case and I was prepared for battle.

During the trial, I was on top of everything. I was poised, professional, and persuasive; I gave it my all. While I wish I could say that at the end of that experience, I prevailed on behalf of my client, won my first trial and shut down that obnoxious opposing attorney, but I can't, because I didn't. The jury returned a verdict in favor of the defendant; because I had lost, my client lost. And the defeat stung – a lot.

Then, a few months later, something truly remarkable happened. After leaving the Court Clerk's Office at the Earle Cabell Federal Courthouse, I ran into the presiding judge in the elevator. Of course, I knew who he was immediately, but I kept my mouth closed (I lost, remember?). After exchanging casual greetings, the look of recognition crossed his face; our resulting conversation went something like this:

Judge: "Oh, I remember you. You were the EEOC lawyer in that pregnancy case a while back."

Me: "Yes, Your Honor. That was me."

Judge: "Yes, yes, I remember your case. You did a great job, a great job."

Me: "Thank you, Your Honor. I was quite nervous. It was my first trial."

Judge: "Well, I never would have known that was your first trial. You did
          an excellent job. The facts weren't really in your favor, but still, you
          did a great job."

Talk about turning a negative into a positive! This exchange with
the judge was the next best outcome I could have ever hoped for. Even
though I did not prevail at trial, I realized I had the most amazing
consolation prizes: earning the respect of my peers and colleagues by
working hard and never giving up; and leaving a lasting positive
impression on a member of the federal bench. I had bloomed.

While it may not have been an enormous bouquet, I learned so
much more in the process. The experience taught me that there will be
times that are challenging; there will be times that are frustrating; and
there will be times when things are difficult and unpleasant. So much so
that you will just want to throw your hands up, give in, and walk away. Of
course, that's always an option, but I learned the hard work comes in
discovering the benefit that could be gained and the lesson that could be
learned by going through this challenging, frustrating, difficult and
unpleasant experience. And the hardest work yields the greatest rewards.

I then began paying much closer attention to those experiences and
became very intentional about identifying some benefit or value (I might
even say, growth) as a result of having gone through the experience. Our
life's journey is really a series of seasons. There is a time and a season for
everything. So, as we realize that we may currently be facing a

challenging season, we must also recognize that it is just that – a season. A finite period of time. What we do during that season, and how we manage the challenges, are up to us.

"Bloom Where You Are Planted" then became a personal mantra of Intentional Positivity for me and my family. Over the years of hearing this mantra, my daughters know immediately what I mean when they are facing a challenge and I share with them that what they're going through may be difficult, but there's something that you must get from this; there's something you should seek to get from this. I tell them to be intentional, otherwise you're going through this pain, misery, and challenge for nothing. And no one has that kind of time to waste. Let's make sure we're going to get something from this, so we can then use the information and lesson to better ourselves, use it to grow, and use it to better the life of someone else.

If you are like me, and you want to grow and continue developing and maturing as an individual, and as a professional, then we must ask ourselves: what is the lesson I need to learn here? What are the tools and skills I need to acquire or refine? What insights can I gain that will better position me for the next challenge? What value can I distill from this particular experience?

Make no mistake, there is some value and benefit in each experience and season. You may not be exactly sure what it is at the time, but know that there is one. The seasons of positive reinforcements are easy to identify when you are getting the accolades, the recognition, and the pats on the back. You're getting a promotion, and the raise, therefore, you can quickly identify the benefits because you are being rewarded. It is infinitely more challenging to look for and embrace the value and benefit in a difficult situation.

Likewise, the transformational thought processes, the mindset and belief systems change, and the internal work that goes along with the "Bloom Where You Are Planted" strategies require commitment, intentionality, authenticity, accountability and periods of discomfort. Your growth will not sprout on its own; you must do the work. When you learn to Bloom Where You Are Planted, you grow through what you go through.

"You have power over your mind – not outside events.
Realize this, and you will find strength." — **Marcus Aurelius**

UNDERSTANDING TRANSFORMATIONAL CHANGE

The key to understanding transformational change, which is the central focus and underlying premise of the Bloom Where You Are Planted strategies, is to recognize that our mental, emotional and physical beings are all tied to the results or outcomes we experience in the world. And to make a meaningful shift in the results or outcomes means that

38

change must also be made within our mental, emotional and physical beings. But, how does one make that change? And changes to what?

SARAH

Sarah is a single, professional young woman in her mid-30s. Even though she has achieved some successes and earned advancements earlier in her career, lately, her supervisor has passed her over the last two times she assigned a team member to lead a special project. Leading a special project usually culminates with some valuable facetime with the department executive, and if the project is successfully executed, that is corporate gold. The last time Sarah led a special project, all the milestone metrics were met – but there was not a lot of buzz generated around the end results – or around Sarah's contributions.

Working 60+ hours a week at the office does not leave time for Sarah to do much of anything else. She doesn't date or develop a circle of friends to build a social life, or work out regularly. She thinks that because she has gained a bit of weight, no one would find her attractive enough to date; in fact, she is convinced that the extra weight is the reason she has not been tapped recently to lead a special project.

Inwardly, Sarah is resentful of those that seem to be moving ahead – in life and on the job. She just doesn't understand why she feels so stuck – and she's looking for a change.

HARPER

Harper is a single, professional young woman in her mid-30s. Even though she, too, has had some successes and advancements earlier in her career, lately, she has been passed over by her supervisor the last two times she assigned a team member to lead a special project. When Harper last led a special project, all the milestone metrics were met – but there was not a lot of buzz generated around the end results – or around Harper, so she went to her supervisor and asked for feedback on what could have made a difference in the way her project was received.

After learning that her last presentation was perceived as lacking in energy and passion, and that the audience was especially disengaged when she read the presentation word-for-word from the PowerPoint slides, Harper volunteered to lead the next project – even though it was considered a lower-profile project, with no likelihood of executive exposure. She managed the project with expert precision, exceeding her supervisor's expectations by bringing in all the deliverables before the deadline. Harper rehearsed and memorized her talking points and delivered an engaging and impactful presentation. She is now in line to lead the next high-profile cross-functional special project.

With this additional work, Harper is working 60+ hours a week at the office but remains very intentional in utilizing her free time – spending it with family and friends. In fact, she met her recent romantic interest at the fitness center, where she started working out to bring down her recent weight gain.

Inwardly, Harper is grateful for the opportunities to demonstrate her presentation and leadership skills and is excited that she is on the path of improving her health and gaining physical strength.

ELEMENTS OF TRANSFORMATIONAL CHANGE

Behavioral scientists and psychologists have confirmed that, as complex, integrated human beings, the thoughts we have or express in our conscious minds press through to our unconscious mind – creating feelings and emotions (energy in motion) that align with those conscious thoughts. This energy in motion (our emotions) drive our actions and behaviors, which then lead to specific results. To put it simply, if you consciously have self-limiting thoughts (you **think** you are inadequate, unworthy, unlovable, undeserving, etc., etc.), a physiological reaction occurs, and you then **feel** 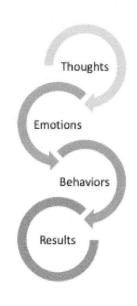 inadequate, unworthy, unlovable, and undeserving. These emotions then drive you to **behave** as if you were inadequate, unworthy, unlovable, or undeserving, which leads to negative and undesirable **results.**

41

Conversely, by embracing self-affirming thoughts (you **think** you are confident, successful and powerful), the physiological reaction produces emotions and **feelings** of confidence, success and power. These emotions drive you to **behave** as a confident, successful and powerful person and to achieve the **results** that confident, successful and powerful people achieve.

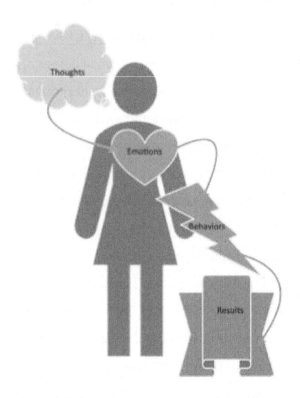

Basically, our thoughts become instant visual images in our brains. In our mind's eye, we can literally "see" ourselves as scared or excited, victorious or defeated, powerful or powerless. Even as you read those words, I bet you got a mental picture of yourself and could see yourself scared, then excited; victorious, then defeated; powerful, then powerless. What's fascinating is that our brain – upon receiving these mental images – interprets them as our current state of being and reacts to prepare the body accordingly by flooding the body with a chemical release that supports the mental images we created. As I learned about these concepts and began to utilize them in my own life – I was truly amazed at how spectacularly we are designed – and how we can use the mechanics of that design for our own benefit.

Before you look at the comparative table for Sarah's and Harper's results – ask yourself: do you identify more closely with Sarah or Harper? Which belief system is more reflective of yours? Have you ever held the thoughts that Sarah had? What about Harper? How did you manage those thoughts? And how did those thoughts make you feel? Would you have done anything differently than either Sarah or Harper? Like what?

Are you satisfied with the results you have been achieving? Is your intuition telling you that you are capable of so much more? Or are you telling yourself that your current situation is as good as it's going to get? Are you ready for a change?

Now, take some time to reflect on the results achieved by Sarah and Harper – based primarily on the thoughts and emotions they experienced in response to a similar set of facts and external events.

Your current life situation is not permanent. You are not stuck. You have choices. You are allowed to grow and change.

	Sarah	Harper
Thoughts	I don't have what it takes to be successful. Everyone else is better than me. I will never get married being this overweight and working these hours.	I am open to learning new skills and improving my performance. I am ready for the next level. I enjoy spending time with my family and friends.
Emotions	I feel inadequate. I feel unattractive. I feel jealous of others who have what I want.	I feel smarter when I learn something new. I feel stronger when I work out.
Behaviors	Does not seek feedback to improve performance; does not attempt to develop new skills or competencies; isolates self from family, friends; declines invitations for dates	Works to demonstrate improved performance; volunteers for new opportunities; collaborates with other team members; commits to exercise/health regimen
Results	Stalled career; limited professional network; lack of social engagements; compromised physical health	Career gains momentum; strong professional relationships; better physical health

MAKING TRANSFORMATIONAL CHANGES:
BE – DO – HAVE

In a session with my life coach, we were discussing the complete mindshift changes that have to a occur when a person, such as myself, transitions from being a professional, seasoned employee to a novice entrepreneur business owner. My transition was hitting a rough patch; I was not feeling productive. I had no blueprint for successfully establishing and running my own coaching and consulting business. What was I supposed to do? How was I going to make this work?

Being an action-oriented, goal-driven person, I was placing my emphasis and focus on what I was doing and accomplishing – or what I felt I was **not** doing and **not** accomplishing. While being action-oriented and goal-driven had served me well in the past – now, as an entrepreneur, focusing so intently on the "doing" as the starting point for building my business was creating a barrier. I had painted myself into a non-productive corner.

I believed I needed to **do** specific things (accomplish predetermined tasks) in order to say I **had** a business and **become** a successful business owner. My focus (DO – HAVE – BE), as we will later discover, was all wrong.

My coach shared with me the BE – DO – HAVE model as a framework for implementing transformational change. It is a simple, yet very powerful tool.

In order to BE the successful business owner, executive coach and consultant, I first had to envision myself as the successful business owner, executive coach and consultant. I had to have a clear picture of who I was, what was important to me, what results I wanted to see, and what beliefs and values were essential components of that visual image of myself as a successful business owner, executive coach and consultant.

By first becoming clear about who and what I wanted to **BE**, I was then better equipped to be intentional on the actions I took and the choices I made **(DO)** to end up with the desired successful outcome **(HAVE)** that aligns with my core values and beliefs.

Here's how it works:

BE:

- Start with the results you desire. Have a very clear mental picture of your goals and what success looks like.

- Ask yourself the following questions:

  o What do I want? Why do I want this?

  o What things are important to me?

  o What am I passionate about?

46

- o What are my beliefs? My values? What do I stand for?

- o Why is this transformational change important to me?

- Next, envision:

  - o Who do I authentically need to be?

  - o What kind of a person would have access to the outcomes I desire?

DO:

- When we have clarity about our authentic selves and those things that are important to us, being intentional about making decisions that align with our authenticity and values becomes simpler.

- In being the kind of person you have envisioned, ask yourself:

  - o What would I be doing?

  - o What are the most important actions I am taking today to accomplish my goals?

  - o What unimportant beliefs do I need to release?

HAVE:

- Evaluate the outcome of your actions.

- Ask yourself:

  o Am I satisfied with the outcome?

  o Do I need to continue on the same path – or refine my approach?

BE your authentic self, where your beliefs drive you to DO the actions that lead you to HAVE the results that you desire and align with your core values.

The order in which these concepts are oriented is critical to making a successful transformational change. Your approach will determine if you would be considered an Underdog, a Workaholic or a Champion. Which one are you?

Let's see:

An Underdog approaches life and transformational change in the **HAVE-DO-BE** order. An Underdog is always waiting for externals to change before they can move ahead in life. They will commonly say:

- When I **HAVE** more time, money and resources, then I'll **DO** the things I've always wanted to, and then I'll **BE** happy and successful. OR:

- When I lose these 20 pounds/get that promotion, then I will go shopping for new clothes/perform at a higher level, and then I will be happy and successful.

- The problem is I don't **HAVE** those things yet. I haven't lost the weight; I haven't been promoted, so I can't be happy.

- If I had what that person over there had, I'd certainly be as successful as them, and then I'd be happy. But, I don't, so I'm not.

A Workaholic (this was me) is focused on the **DO-HAVE-BE** approach to life. The Workaholic draws a direct causal connection between the amount of work or activity they engage in and their success. They say:

- The more I **DO,** the more I will **HAVE**. The more I **HAVE**, the happier I'll **BE**.

- The problem is, the more I do, the more there is still to do – and the more I have, there is still more to have.

- I am defined by what I do – I am driven, busy and tired. I am Woman. I am Invincible. I am Exhausted.

- The more I have, the more there is to lose, so I must work harder.

A Champion of transformational change embraces the **BE-DO-HAVE** order. The Champion does the hard work of self-reflection to know and embrace their authentic selves; to make decisions in line with their beliefs and values; and to make the necessary adjustments and refinements in their actions to continuously improve their satisfaction with the results.

I Am A Champion. You Are a Champion. We Are Champions.

DIGGING DEEPER

PREPARE YOUR SEEDS – CHOOSE YOR TOOLS

Set the Stage for Transformational Change

BE

DO

**Reflect on Your
BE – DO – HAVE**

HAVE

Chapter 3: PLANT YOUR BEST SEEDS
Cultivate An Attitude of Gratitude

"The best way to show my gratitude is to accept everything, even my problems, with joy." – **Mother Theresa**

THE POWER OF GRATITUDE

Gratitude, when exercised consistently, has been known to have tremendous positive mind and bodily effects.

- Gratitude acts as a supernatural shield against negativity
- Gratitude makes you at least 25% happier
- Gratitude rewires your brain, promoting healthier, more positive thoughts
- Gratitude reduces and can eliminate stress
- Gratitude has healing properties
- Gratitude helps improve rest during sleep
- Gratitude boosts self-esteem and performance

- Gratitude improves interpersonal relationships[1]

If we do not feel grateful for what we already have, what makes us think will be happy with more?

Scientific studies have shown that an *"Attitude of Gratitude"* is a beneficial and powerful choice for many reasons: we are healthier; we are happier and more optimistic; it costs nothing; and, requires no special training and very little effort to practice. But, more than that, gratitude also improves your productivity and results, and is an essential component of the ***Bloom Where You Are Planted*** framework:

Gratitude attracts what we want. We attract into our life the things we think about and focus on. What are you currently attracting into your life? Is it peace and prosperity or chaos and scarcity? Are you thinking about possibilities and solutions or barriers and problems? Think about what you do have, rather than focusing on what you don't have. When you are consciously aware of your blessings, and are grateful for them, you are focusing more clearly on what you do want in your life – and are attracting more of those things into your life.

---

[1] Legal disclaimer: The statements have not been evaluated by the Food and Drug Administration, and are not intended to diagnose, treat, cure or prevent any disease.

Gratitude improves relationships. Everyone loves to feel appreciated. We feel good when we know that our efforts, thoughts and deeds are valued and appreciated by others; we get a warm, glowing feeling – and we have the ability to make others feel the same when we show them our appreciation. And it is so easy to do. In fact, I venture to guess we were all taught as children the importance and necessity of saying "thank you."

Be grateful for people, their contributions, their talents and their actions – and make sure you let them know how you feel.

Gratitude reduces negativity. It is hard to be negative about your situation when you are thinking about things for which you are grateful. You may not be crazy about your job – and really despise one of your co-workers, but you made it past the last round of corporate layoffs and you still have a job. You may not drive the fanciest, latest model sportscar, but your sedan is very reliable and gets you where you need to go.

Gratitude helps us learn. Every dark cloud has a silver lining. Behind every problem lies an opportunity. Being grateful for our situation – even if we don't like everything about it – allows us to be thankful for the opportunity to learn something new.

Since gratitude has the ability to make us happier, healthier, more optimistic and more productive, and costs nothing and requires no special training and very little effort to use, why are we not more grateful in our daily lives? What is holding us back? Are we too busy? Do we feel overwhelmed with the demands of our careers, family and other obligations to take a few moments to pause and express appreciation for the things that we do have? How much does it really cost to say, "Thank you?" How many of us take the time to routinely (or even, randomly) consider what we are truly and deeply grateful for?

To truly Bloom Where You Are Planted, you must embrace the fact that now, at this moment, you are more than enough. There is nothing wrong with having dreams and aspirations to grow, evolve and achieve big things – really, really big things. But don't forget: in the midst of your dreams and aspirations, it is important to appreciate and be thankful for where you are at this moment in your journey.

"Gratitude unlocks the fullness of life. It turns what we have into enough and more. It turns denial into acceptance. Chaos to order. Confusion to clarity. You can turn a meal into a feast. A house into a home. A stranger into a friend. Gratitude makes sense of our past, brings peace for today, and creates a vision for tomorrow." - **Melody Beattie**

DEMONSTRATE GRATITUDE– DAILY

We know that gratitude is an attitude, and that we have the choice to express gratitude. Gratitude is also a habit. When we consciously practice being grateful for the people, situations and resources around us, we begin to attract better relationships and results. The habit will be strengthened as you make the choice each day to focus on your blessings and to express genuine gratitude for the things you have.

If you do not already have a journal, I invite you to invest in one – it doesn't have be bound in English leather – a composition book from your local discount store will do the trick. Whatever option you choose, label it as your Daily Gratitude Journal. Choose a time, optimally at the end of the day, when you can spend a few minutes reflecting on the day's events: people you encountered and experiences and thoughts you had. Make a note of the 3 – 5 things that you appreciate and for which you are grateful. You don't have to write a novel, or even use complete sentences. This is your personal journal – no one is judging you on its contents. Simply write down what comes to mind. For example, a sample entry could read:

Today, I am grateful/thankful for . . ..

  Friends that have turned into family

  Each day bringing a brand-new opportunity to start anew

  God's unconditional love

  The roof over my head

As you make your list, spend some time basking in those positive thoughts, and be sure to share that thankfulness with others. This daily exercise of listing the things for which you are grateful and sharing your appreciation with others further cultivates your attitude of gratitude.

What Are You Truly and Deeply Grateful For Right Now?

1. Make a list of five things you are grateful for right now. These can be big things (like your family) or little things (like the fact that someone held the door open for you this morning). This can be a mental list or written down. Do it now.

2. Reflect on your list and allow yourself to feel good about each of your gratitude entries.

3. If there is a person you can thank or show your appreciation to, do that now, too (a quick call or email is a good start!).

Note: You don't have to limit your gratitude list to only five things. Be sure to continue this practice and keep a running summary in your Daily Gratitude Journal.

Gratitude, like faith, is a muscle. The more you use it – the stronger it grows and the more power you have to use it on your behalf. – **Alan Cohen**

DIGGING DEEPER

PLANT YOUR BEST SEEDS – CULTIVATE AN ATTITUDE OF GRATITUDE

BE THANKFUL

"Be thankful that you don't already have everything you desire,

If you did, what would there be to look forward to?

Be thankful when you don't know something

For it gives you the opportunity to learn.

Be thankful for the difficult times.

During those times you grow.

Be thankful for your limitations

Because they give you opportunities for improvement.

Be thankful for each new challenge

Because it will build your strength and character.

Be thankful for your mistakes

They will teach you valuable lessons.

Be thankful when you're tired and weary

Because it means you've made a difference.

It is easy to be thankful for the good things.

A life of rich fulfillment comes to those who are

also thankful for the setbacks.

GRATITUDE can turn a negative into a positive.

Find a way to be thankful for your troubles

and they can become your blessings." ~ Author Unknown

THE 30-DAY GRATITUDE CHALLENGE

*Be Intentional About Being Grateful
*Take the 30-Day Gratitude Challenge
*Use the prompts to guide your reflections of gratitude and record your thoughts in your Daily Gratitude Journal

SUN	MON	TUES	WED
Starting This Challenge	Something You Like About Yourself	A Challenge You Have Overcome	Something You Created
Something Beautiful You Saw Today	Your Spouse or Significant Other	Something You Are Looking Forward To	Your Health And Well-Being
Something You Use Every Day	Someone Who Inspires You	A Personal Talent You Possess	Your Past Experiences
Your Favorite Memory	Opportunities You've Been Given	Someone You've Met	Something You Like About The Current Season
Something You Love	Something That Made You Laugh	Something You Can't Live Without	

Be thankful for each new challenge. Each one works to build your strength and define your character.

THURS	FRI	SAT
Your Greatest Accomplishment	Something You Often Take For Granted	Your Best Personality Trait
Something You Like About Your Job	A Lesson Learned From a Mistake You Made	Family and Friends
Something That Makes You Smile	Something You Like About Your Home	Something Awesome About Your Age
Your Favorite Physical Trait	Something That Has Made You Stronger	A Gift You Have Received
BONUS:	**How You Feel At The End**	**Of This Challenge**

The more you thank life; the more life gives you to be thankful for.

Bloom Where You Are Planted

Chapter 4: CREATE AN ENRICHED ENVIRONMENT
Nourish Your Growth With A Positive Attitude

"If you don't like something, change it; if you can't change it, change your attitude about it." ~*Maya Angelou*

THE POWER OF A POSITIVE ATTITUDE

Similar to the results and benefits of practicing gratitude, studies have shown that positivity attracts positivity, and people who embrace a positive attitude are:

- Much more productive in the workplace

- Much more likely to be noticed by their boss

- Much more likely to be recognized for an opportunity when it comes up

Bloom Where You Are Planted

It really doesn't take a rocket scientist or someone with an advanced degree in psychology to recognize the effects and power of a positive attitude. So, why is having a positive attitude so difficult for so many people? Is it because the burdens of our responsibilities in our daily lives weigh us down and make us cynical? I get it; it makes sense. Sometimes, it's the fact that those folks who are generally and consistently happy and positive, can get a bad rap. They are often labeled as naïve, a Pollyanna, or someone who is out of touch with reality.

Other times, it's the fact that after getting two small children or even one teenager up and out of bed, faces washed, teeth brushed, hair combed, appropriately clothed, fed and out the door for school, with all of the required completed homework, permission slips and equipment for their after-school extracurricular activities; then you've got to fight the morning rush-hour traffic, which wouldn't be complete without a stalled car blocking a lane, arrive to the office in the nick of time before your micromanaging boss asks to see the report that she only requested at 8:00 p.m. the night before – all before having your morning cup of coffee or other caffeine of choice, who's really in the mood to project a positive attitude? Am I right?

Yet, even if you have the most cooperative children, a hassle-free commute to shuttle off to school or have to fight a traffic jam on your way to work or the best boss ever, there are countless other sources of stress and negativity that surround us on a daily basis. All you need to do is turn on the television – from the news networks' coverage of current events to politics, the economy, entertainment and popular culture – we are bombarded by negative images, conversations and behaviors.

Being surrounded by negative messages, cynicism, low self-images and negative self-talk, we have become so insulated against positivity, that it is hard to share and receive positive feedback. I have witnessed time and time again how people struggle with giving someone a compliment. For some reason, they have rationalized that if they compliment someone else on their appearance, intelligence, or performance, that it is somehow an indictment against their own appearance, intelligence or performance.

In other words: If I say something nice about you, that means there is something wrong with me by comparison. What's even worse is our own inability to receive a compliment from someone else. If we are told that we have on a nice dress, or that our hair looks good, or we did a great job on the presentation, we find some way to diminish, disregard and downright dispute the feedback, rather than simply saying, "Thank you." We are falling out of practice of sharing positive messages with others and with ourselves.

Because of this phenomenon, whenever I speak to different groups and organizations to share any aspect of the **Bloom Where You Are Planted** philosophy and its strategies, I always include a section on positivity and the need for positive affirmations. I generally lead off this part of the discussion by asking the audience how many use positive affirmations, and how frequently. I am no longer surprised by the number of people who do not raise their hands. We simply are not connected to the process of speaking positivity into our own lives. Next, I challenge the group to offer a compliment to the individual sitting on either side of them, regardless of whether or not they know each other. (Think of the instructions often given in church: "Turn to your neighbor and say, 'Neighbor'" . . . . .).

They need only identify one characteristic upon which to share something nice. And if they don't already know the person – it's usually something external and superficial, like: Your hair looks nice. You have a nice smile. Or, I love those shoes. Even if it is a compliment on something superficial, it has the amazing effect of causing people to smile, as the exercise breaks down walls and brings people closer together. It's a start.

POSITIVE EXPRESSIONS THAT ACTIVATE LIFE (PETAL)

Next, I hand out a card and ask everyone to take the time to write down 3 to 5 positive affirmation for themselves. I provide examples that remind and empower them to embrace the value that they bring, who they are, and why they are so awesome. They are asked to write down an affirmation, and to then speak their affirmations out loud. Much like cultivating the attitude of gratitude, when we speak affirmations to ourselves, we see ourselves in that way and we start to internalize and believe the affirmations to be true. We are then able to act and operate in

66

the light that is consistent with those affirmations. As we say them, we use them, we post them, we continue the practice of positivity.

Research has shown that the continued practice of positivity though self-affirmation leads to boosted problem-solving skills, especially when under pressure or stress. This can be particularly helpful in elevating your performance and your presence in the workplace and in other social settings. Positive self-affirmations make you more aware of your thought processes. And greater <u>awareness</u> makes you more likely to challenge negative thoughts as they arise. This also enhances your self-knowledge, helping you to know what you really want in life.

Let's not forget that positive self-affirmations are also directly connected with your feelings of gratefulness and your attitude of gratitude, which enhances your perspective and allows you to more intentionally focus on the good things in life.

In summary, it is a proven fact that, by changing the way you think, you can transform your whole life – and bloom wherever you are.

Now it's your turn. I invite you to use the space below to list five positive self-affirmations. Five positive expressions about yourself that you can use as a source of encouragement and inspiration. But before you do, I want to make sure that each affirmation is styled as an "I am . . ." statement.

Being positive in a negative situation is not naïve. It's leadership.

THE POWER OF I AM

Why? Because the two most powerful words in the English language are **I AM.** Whatever follows your "I Am" statement follows you and manifests itself in your life; be it success or failure, pain or joy, victory or defeat. Think about the "I Am" statements we declare every day – most times, without even being mindful of the energy we are putting in the universe, the visual images we are sending our brains or how we are calling forth the very outcome we have declared.

How many times have you said: "I am so old," or "I am not smart/talented enough" or "I am not pretty/funny/brave like _____" or " I am broke/tired." You are handing each of these negative thoughts an invitation to come and find you and to take up residence in your life – to ensure that you look and feel old; that you don't act or speak like a smart person; that you never have the confidence to display your talents. And on and on. You get the picture.

What is so amazing, though, is that you – and only you – are in charge of what follows your "I Am" statements. You get to choose. What do you want to manifest in your life? Is it health, strength, prosperity, freedom, courage, wisdom? Then, speak it. Claim it. Own it. How much will your life transform if you change the way you speak to and about yourself? How much would your life change if you were mindful of the invitations that you were extending and the future you were creating?

Imagine now, what would happen in your life if you were to say to yourself:

"I am beautiful."

"I am powerful and strong."

"I am love."

"I am wise."

"I am able."

"I am brave."

"I am better today than I was yesterday."

Let me tell you something: you will start to **think** that you are what you say you are – your thoughts will inform your emotions and you will begin to **feel** that you are what you say you are – and your feelings will guide your behaviors and you will **act** as you who you have said you are, and the **outcome** of your actions will reflect the results you brought into existence.

Now that you know about the power of I AM – list your PETALS of Power affirmations here:

_____

_____

_____

_____

_____

_____

I am in charge of how I feel, and today I am choosing happiness.

USE YOUR POSITIVE ATTITUDE TO DISPEL NEGATIVITY

We are surrounded by so much negativity, and when those negative thoughts arise, we have to be prepared to overcome them. Oftentimes, the negativity is internal, because of how we talk to ourselves – our internal dialog. We tell ourselves we're not good enough, that we don't deserve it, or that we are not smart enough for that next role.

Then, there are the external sources. Other people telling us that we are not ready, or that we are not good/smart/pretty/tough/creative enough. Someone always seems to have something negative to say. I'm reminded of a quote from one of my favorite movies, *Steel Magnolias,* in which Clairee proudly proclaims, "If you can't say anything nice about anybody, then come sit by me."

These are the people who thrive on negativity, strife and discord. If trouble isn't brewing around them – then, they will stir some up. Keep in mind, though: if you are committed to transformational change and taking the journey to **Bloom Where You Are Planted**, then you must also be committed to limiting your exposure to negative influences and to using the energy of your positive attitude to dispel any negativity that may find you.

70

So, you must be prepared to handle those negative thoughts. And your first response should be with an affirmation, such as,"Oh, yes, I am good enough;" or "You know what – I am smart and I can totally do this job like a rock star;" or "Regardless of the number on the scale, I am beautiful and I love the skin I am in." That is the starting point. When we exercise the muscle of speaking life into ourselves, we nourish our body, mind and soul with positivity rather than negativity.

TURN YOUR NEGATIVES INTO POSITIVES

As I was scrolling through my daily news feed recently, I stumbled upon this human-interest story. While it made me question the motivation of strangers, it also reinforced my belief that at our core, there is love and compassion.

A woman eating lunch at a McDonald's in Georgia took a photo of a young man sleeping in one of the booths and uploaded the image to Facebook. In her post, she noted that when she complained to the manager about this man sleeping in the dining area, she was informed that management was aware of the situation and had no objection to his presence. While I am not certain of the outcome this woman had in mind, the compassionate response from the McDonald's employee was NOT IT. Dissatisfied and angry with the employee's response, as evidenced by the angry-faced emoji she used to end her commentary, the woman remarked in her post that this incident was another reason to move away from her Georgia town.

Bloom Where You Are Planted

Whether or not this woman posted the picture of the sleeping man, along with her interaction, her feelings, the social commentary – to intentionally shame this man or to make herself feel better about her status in life or to give her "friends" some time to gnaw on and also express their displeasure – is unknown. But one of her friends shared that post and the community took notice and responded in such a resounding manner that it left NO DOUBT how they felt about this young man.

As it turns out, this individual, Mr. C., was a homeless 21-year-old single father of an infant son. He had been sleeping in the booth at that particular McDonald's – unbothered by the staff (and other patrons/customers) – because he worked there and was merely trying to get some rest between his shifts. He stated that his life had taken a downward turn after recently losing his mother; however, he was determined to make whatever sacrifices were necessary to work and provide for his son. Those sacrifices included sleeping in a booth at a public fast food establishment.

Those who saw the post made it clear that they were in the community of love and support. When he came back to work at McDonald's the day after the post, he was astonished to find that his community had donated diapers, baby clothes and other supplies. Someone donated a hotel room for Mr. C. and his son. A local business owner lent Mr. C. a car so that he could have transportation to the many job offers he had received, and a barber gave him a free haircut so he could look his best on his interviews.

When asked how he felt about the woman posting his picture, he stated that originally he was a little upset at her, and he assumed that no one would actually care. But he stated he had no ill will toward this woman because now, thanks to her and her post, he is no longer homeless. He's no longer sleeping in a restaurant booth. He now has an opportunity to make a fresh start and work, to care for and provide for the young son he's raising. He sees it as a blessing.

That's a clear example of Blooming Where You Are Planted; taking the negatives and turning them into positives so that it benefits you. Mr. C. did it, and so can you.

Be bold and brave enough to know that even if you are in the middle of a storm or facing a negative challenge, there is always something positive either in that situation or that will come from that negative situation. Look for it and be prepared to embrace it when it appears.

You have survived everything that life has thrown at you so far. That is a 100% success rate. There is no doubt you can handle whatever may come tomorrow.

THE UNIVERSITY OF ALABAMA

As a native of Alabama and a graduate of the University of Alabama, one of the most powerful and life-changing illustrations of turning around a negative situation occurred on June 11, 1963, when black students Vivian Malone Jones and James Hood enrolled in the then all-white University of Alabama.

To gain   her enrollment, it was necessary for Ms. Jones to sue the University and have her case heard and adjudicated in her favor by a federal court. The White House had to send National Guard troops to the campus to ensure her safety.

And if that wasn't enough, there was one more uphill battle ahead. One that would define an era and forever change the course of history in the state of Alabama. In order to register for the collegiate classes at the institution for which she had been legally admitted, Ms. Jones had to defy the Governor of Alabama, George Wallace, as he blocked the entrance to Foster Auditorium to refuse her admission. This televised standoff became known as, "The Stand in the Schoolhouse Door," memorializing, before an international audience, Wallace's hateful and oppositional sentiments with his signature slogan: "Segregation now, segregation tomorrow, segregation forever."

Yet, Ms. Jones persisted. When asked about her bravery to do what she did on that day, during the height of the Civil Rights Movement, and just one day before Mississippi activist Medgar Evers was assassinated in his driveway, Vivian Malone Jones had this to say: "My mind was mostly on going to class and doing the best I could. It had taken me two and a half years to gain admission, and nobody – including the governor – was going to tell me I didn't have the right to attend that school."

Unfortunately, due to the hostility and negative attitude displayed by protesting students, Hood transferred a short time later to an out-of-state university in Detroit, leaving Ms. Jones as the only black student on the campus for that school year. Undeterred, she remained; and in the spring of 1965, Vivian Malone Jones made history by becoming the first black graduate of the University of Alabama, earning a B.S. degree in Business Administration.

Jones used her experience as a platform to motivate and encourage students to always be ready to make a difference – because at any point, they might be called upon to be bold and courageous as they walk toward a negative situation that could ultimately lead to opportunities for others.

In 2000, the University saluted her life accomplishments with an honorary Doctor of Humane Letters, and in 2010, the University honored Jones' lasting impact on the Capstone again by dedicating the plaza in front of Foster Auditorium in her name. Today, Malone-Hood Plaza serves as a lasting tribute to Jones' courage, determination and grace. And I, and countless others who stood on her shoulders as we graced the historic halls and picturesque grounds of the University of Alabama, in our unchallenged pursuit and attainment of higher education, owe her a deep debt of gratitude. ***Roll Tide!!***

Be bold and brave enough to know that even if you are in the middle of a storm or facing a negative and daunting challenge, that there is always something positive either in that situation or that will come from that negative situation. Look for it and be prepared to embrace it when it appears.

You may not control all the events that happen to you, but you can decide not to be reduced by them. – Maya Angelou

BE INTENTIONAL ABOUT BEING POSITIVE

Having a positive attitude also impacts the words that you use. Words matter. Change the negative to a positive. Be aware of the messages that you communicate. For example, try substituting some of the more positive language below – even when you are expressing a feeling or emotion that's not so positive.

Negative	Positive
Disgusted	Surprised
Exhausted	In need of a recharge
I hate/don't like. .	I prefer
Overwhelmed	In demand
Weird	Unique
Criticism	Feedback/Advice/Guidance
Problem	Challenge
Sorry	Regret

Find positive words for school, friends, work, love, and life. Thinking of what's positive will keep your mind on what is good. You will find more blessings and opportunities in your life and not worry about the bad. Positive words will give you motivation to try new things.

Ten of the Most Positive Words

Beautiful: delighting the senses or exciting intellectual or emotional admiration. Beautiful is all encompassing, organic and whole.

Invoking the physical, spiritual, and emotional realms of our being, Beautiful is far more powerful than gorgeous, stunning, or lovely.

78

Friend: a person you know well and regard with affection and trust.

Whether for a reason, a season or a lifetime, friends help us cope with challenges, motivate our best work and celebrate life. Friendships sustain and nourish.

Forgiveness: the act of excusing a mistake or offense; a compassionate feeling that supports a willingness to forgive. Forgiveness is one of the most powerful, and sometimes the most difficult, responses that we could ever have. Forgiving others who have harmed us or those we hold dear can be very hard.

There is perhaps no greater demonstration of faith and positivity than showing love, grace and mercy, combined with having a heart that knows the power of forgiveness and deciding to use that power to release someone else from the pain and hurt they have caused.

Gratitude: a feeling of thankfulness and appreciation.

Happiness: a state of well-being characterized by emotions ranging from contentment to intense joy.

Happiness is more than just a positive attitude or being in a good mood. Happiness comes from a deep sense of well-being that allows a person to be happy regardless of external circumstances.

Joy: the emotion of great happiness. It has a deeper/different implication than "happiness," which is looked upon as situational.

When we are joyful, it shows. We can even experience Joy in the midst of sorrow or a negative situation and lift up others around us. Joy makes us stronger – inside and out.

Laughter: the activity of laughing.

Laughter is strong medicine. It draws people together in ways that trigger healthy physical and emotional changes in the body. Laughter strengthens your immune system, boosts your mood, diminishes pain, and protects you from the damaging effects of stress.

Love: a strong positive emotion of regard and affection.

Love can create life; keep us going throughout life; is what remains after life. Love brings people together and connects us at our deepest cellular level – at our core. Love is the most fundamentally nurturing force in nature. With it – we thrive, we produce, we excel, we conquer, we overcome. Without it – we wither, we isolate ourselves, we destroy.

Patience: good-natured tolerance of delay or incompetence.

Patience as an active choice to hold tight until intuition says, "make your move." It means waiting your turn, knowing your turn will come. Patience is a strength and a virtue.

Whereas frustration focuses on externals, patience draws inward towards a greater wisdom and lets you intuit the situation to get a larger, more loving view to determine the right course of action. Practicing patience will help you dissipate stress and give you a choice about how you respond to disappointment and frustration. When you can stay calm, centered and not act rashly out of frustration, all areas of your life will improve.

Peace: A divine state of consciousness – a sense of calm – deeply felt mentally and spiritually – even in the face of adversity and discord. (A peace that passeth all understanding: God will bless you with peace that no one can completely understand. And that peace will control how you think and feel. (Philippians 4:7)

To Practice Peace:

Be Selective with Your Time: Stop trying to do everything. Multitasking robs you of your peace.

Learn to Say No: Taking on too much because of discomfort in saying No; not wanting to disappoint; always wanting to please; searching for approval; constantly putting others' needs/desires ahead of our own, to your detriment robs you of your peace. Other ways to say No include: "I am not able to commit to that right now." "No, I can't do that – but here is what I can do."

Give yourself permission/grace not to be perfect: Use the paper plates; feed the kids fast food; save the laundry for the weekend or until next week. There is no need to subject yourself to trying to attain the unattainable. Attempting perfection robs you of your peace. Do the best you can – when you can – and let the rest of it go, guilt-free.

Resist Procrastination: Get started. Take the first step; get the hard stuff out of the way first. Establish accountability to avoid delay when beginning projects. Eliminate distractions that can derail you or prevent you from beginning or finishing your work. Procrastination feeds stress, and stress definitely robs you of your peace

DIGGING DEEPER:

CREATE AN ENRICHED ENVIRONMENT – NOURISH YOUR GROWTH WITH A POSITIVE ATTITUDE

As you work to develop a more organic, holistic and positive attitude, keep the following points in mind. Bookmark this page and come back to it as often as you need.

❀   You owe yourself the love that you so freely give to other people.

❀   Your body hears everything your mind says. Keep it positive.

❀ You are enough. Who you are is enough. What you do is enough. And what you have is enough.

❀ Do not allow the behavior of others to destroy your inner peace.

❀ What you think – you become. What you feel – you attract. What you imagine – you create.

❀ What others think of me is their choice. What I think of myself is my choice. I am only responsible for my choices.

❀ When a negative thought comes up, do the following:

    o **Ask** yourself these questions:

        ▪ Do I believe this thought? Why? Is it factual or do I just believe it to be true?

- Where is this thought coming from? Is it mine or from someone else?
- How long have I held this belief? Does it still serve me? Am I ready to release this belief and heal?

o **Visualize** a positive solution instead. Remember, your brain will think it's real.

o **Change** your pattern of negative thinking by adding a new routine such as daily journaling your reflections of gratitude and positive self-affirming "I am" statements.

"You've been criticizing yourself for years and it hasn't worked out well for you. Try approving yourself and see what happens." – **Louise Hay**

Chapter 5: ESTABLISH FIRM ROOTS
Be the Change. Do the Work. Have the Desired Outcome.

Your life only gets better when you do. Work on yourself and the rest will follow.

SET YOUR INTENTIONS

Here's a bit of irony: the title of this book, and the basis for my executive coaching and leadership development programs, is, of course, ***"Bloom Where You Are Planted;"*** yet, I do not have a green thumb – I mean, at all. At best, I can identify and name some of my favorite flowers: rose; tulip; hydrangea; lily; hibiscus. And, that's about it.

On the other hand, however, my sister, who has a natural green thumb and actually finds gardening to be relaxing, can not only name all the different varieties of roses and pretty purple and yellow flowers, she also knows the time of year to plant which variety of them. Her yard *always* looks amazing!

Bloom Where You Are Planted

On my first-ever horticultural endeavor, I planted tulips. I was so proud of myself for even attempting to grow anything; I even purchased one of those special tulip bulb hole digger things to dig the holes to drop in the bulbs. Well, I didn't realize until after I had planted all the bulbs, that I had actually planted them upside down – every last one of them. Who knew there was such a thing? (Yes, my sister did!) Yet, even though I planted the bulbs upside down, do you know what happened? Spring rolled around and the tulips bloomed anyway.

Not only did they bloom that spring, they continued to bloom – year after year – despite the environment I created for them. Despite the less-than-ideal situation in which I planted those tulips, they still bloomed. Keep in mind, that you – just like those tulips – already possess everything you need to bloom, regardless of the conditions of your environment.

As we move to the next phase of the **Bloom Where You Are Planted** framework, we should take a moment to reflect on having already laid the foundation for us to **BE** the change we want to see by cultivating deeper gratitude and planting seeds of positivity. And we know that if we truly desire to experience a different outcome, we must get to the root of the matter and effectuate a transformational change in our beliefs, our thoughts and our behaviors.

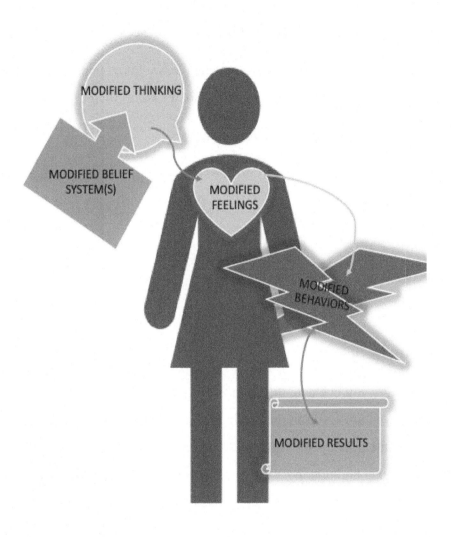

"Be the change you want to see in the world." –Mahatma Gandhi

Set Your Intentions: See the Outcome You Seek

As Champions of transformational change, we know that a successful journey begins with the end in mind. So, let's start there.

-What do you see in your future?

-What do you WANT to see? (How would you like to see yourself in the future?)

-What will it take to get there?

Assess Your Current Situation

Self-Assessment (How do I see myself?)

Self-Reflection

As you evaluate the environment you are currently in, and the results you are currently producing, make a determination as to whether it is something that is pleasing and productive or whether it is negative, challenging and no longer serving its purpose. If your current situation is in need of a change, what is the cause of your dissatisfaction or frustration or unhappiness? What is the source? Is your frustration centered around your job, your family, your friends, your spouse or your health?

For example, do you feel that you are not advancing fast enough at work? And, if so, is it true that your career is stalling, or do you just believe that it is? If your career has actually hit a roadblock, what happened? Have you been meeting all of your performance metrics? Do

88

you still have the exposure to the right people? Do you lack the necessary skills and experience or relationships to take it to the next level? Do you possess the skill set and behavioral competencies that are valued by your employer? Do you even know what they are? Are they aligned with what you can actually contribute? If you don't know the company's culture and the competencies, skills, and behaviors that it values, your goal is to find out what they are and then determine whether what your company stands for and aligns with is, in fact, what you stand for.

It could be that you have been going overboard to prove to your boss that you are the best, but what your boss really looks for is how well you interact with your fellow team members. Whereas your company really values relationships, and spending time with people, you don't have time to do that because you have been working too hard. Therefore, you rarely come out of your office to speak to anyone, and you don't ask your colleagues about their weekends. Quite frankly, you don't care how their weekend was.

In such a scenario, it really would not matter if you are knocking out 10- to 12-hour workdays, and consistently overdelivering stellar work products; your employer may not see you as a cultural fit in their organization. Therefore, you're not being promoted because they're not going to put you in a position to manage a team where you have the ability to influence and manage others if you aren't able to demonstrate and model what is of value to them.

Bloom Where You Are Planted

"One of the lessons that I grew up with was to always stay true to yourself and never let what somebody else says distract you from your goals. And so, when I hear about negative and false attacks, I really don't invest any energy in them, because I know who I am." ~
Michelle Obama

The above hypothetical underscores the necessity in you knowing and understanding your authentic self, your values and beliefs so that you can make the best-informed decision on the actions you need to take that align with those beliefs. In order to obtain that deep understanding, a self-assessment is in order. Through the Internal Assessment, below, you will get a better understanding of your belief systems and values. You will explore what you are passionate about and discover your strengths and weaknesses.

Your responses to the Internal Assessment questions below will give you a clear mental picture of your goals and what success looks like.

As a second component to these reflection exercises, I have also included an external assessment, to be shared with others to seek their feedback on their impressions and observations of you. You will end up with a picture of not only how you see you – but how others see you as well.

Consolidating the results of these assessments will reveal information that is commonly known about you as well as some private information and blind spots. From there, you can become laser focused on

90

what modifications to your beliefs and thoughts are necessary to drive the different actions and behaviors you need to perform in order to achieve your desired results.

Take your time as you go through these assessments. This is not a race and you are not on anyone else's timetable but your own. Give yourself grace and space as you work through the self-reflection exercises.

Be truthful and transparent in your responses. Encourage those you have selected to provide their feedback on your external assessment to do the same.

SELF-ASSESSMENT

Ten Questions in each category below – not intended to be an exhaustive list – but it is just enough to get you started on the introspective journey of self-reflection.

YOUR GIFTS AND TALENTS

1. Use 10 words to describe yourself – as you see yourself today.

2. Use 10 words to describe your IDEAL SELF.

3. What do you love most about yourself?

4. What would you say are your special talents, skills or abilities?

5. How do you use them?

6. What activities are you engaged in when you feel the most connected to your gifts and talents?

7. What special talents skills or abilities do you not embrace? This is an area where you frequently receive compliments – but for some reason, you always diminish its value or its effect on others.

8. What's holding you back from embracing your brilliant gifts? Why are you doing this?

9. What would be different if you made a conscious decision NOT to diminish your gifts?

10. How do you think your family and friends would describe you?

(a) Would your work colleagues' description of you mirror that given by your family and friends?

YOUR AREAS OF VULNERABILITY

1. What do you really not like about yourself?

2. What feedback have you received from others on areas you could improve within your life? How did you respond to that feedback?

3. Did you make any changes or adjustments in your life based on that feedback? Why or why not?

4. What's holding you back from being your IDEAL SELF today?

5. What would you do if fear were not a factor?

    a. What is the basis of that fear? What's behind it?

6. Describe five (5) situations in which you accomplished a particular task – even though you were afraid. For each situation, describe:

    a. how you convinced yourself to start the task; and

    b. how you felt when you completed the task.

7. If you had a magic wand and could go back in time, list the top five (5) things you would do differently. This could be something you said or didn't say; something you did or didn't do. Why do you want a "do-over" for these choices?

8. When was the last time you did something for "the first time?"

9. Would you watch a sad movie, knowing it will make you cry? Or do you avoid sad movies at all costs?

    a. If you say, "It depends;" then, when would you knowingly watch or actively avoid watching a sad movie?

10. As you think about your personal growth and development, do you find it more effective to focus your efforts on maximizing your strengths (by paying less attention to the areas where development is needed) or on minimizing the areas of development (by paying less attention to your strengths)?

YOUR VALUES AND BELIEFS

1. What are your fundamental beliefs and core values?

2. How would you define your Life's Purpose? What do you feel led/called to do with your time, talents and resources?

3. Are you actively pursuing your Life's Purpose today? If not, why not?

4. Do you wake up every morning feeling excited?

5. Who and what drives/motivates you?

6. Name five people you admire for being successful.

    a. In your eyes, what is it about them that makes them successful?

7. What activities have meaning and heart for you?

8. How much time do you have to spend engaging in these activities?

9. What are you most grateful for? Why?

10. What thoughts or beliefs do you hold about yourself? About your talents? Your areas of vulnerability?

    a. Where did they come from? (Internal; External; Not sure)

    b. How long have you held these beliefs about yourself? (Always known; Gradually acquired over time; Recent acquisition)

    c. Are these thoughts and beliefs positive and affirming? Do they work to your advantage and keep you moving forward?

    d. Are these thoughts beliefs negative and demeaning?

        1) Do they work to your disadvantage and hold you back?

        2) If these thoughts and beliefs are negative and demeaning – and holding you back – why are you holding on to them?

YOUR RELATIONSHIPS WITH OTHERS:

1. What is most important to you in a relationship?

2. How can others have a positive relationship with you – what do you need most?

3. How do you express emotion in your interpersonal relationships?

    a. Do you let it all hang out? Does everybody know exactly how you feel at all times?

    1) Why?

    2) What have been the consequences (positive and negative) of your emotional expressions?

  b. Do you hold it in? Are folks are often wondering what you're thinking about and how you're feeling?

    1) Why?

    2) What have been the consequences (positive and negative) of you suppressing your emotional expressions?

4. Is there someone who has wronged you that you need to forgive – but you just haven't been able to take that step? Looking beyond the pain you endured, what's holding you back from forgiving this person?

5. What do you do when you are faced with interacting with a person you find challenging or difficult?

6. How do you feel when others in your circle succeed or are celebrated for their accomplishments?

7. How often do you eat lunch alone? On the occasions that you do eat lunch alone, is it intentional or situational?

8. What really makes you angry?

  a. What are those triggers?

  b. How do you deal with the anger?

9. Does spending time with a lot of people energize you? Or does it drain you?

10. Does meeting new people in an unfamiliar setting excite and energize you? Or does it make you want to run and hide?

DESTINY AND LEGACY

1. What does your ideal vision for your life look like?

2. How are you living "your best life?"

3. What is your biggest goal – from a personal perspective?

4. What obstacle or barrier is between you and your biggest goal?

5. What do you have to do to remove this barrier (or at least to get over it or around it)?

6. How do you envision leaving an impact on the world? What does your legacy look like?

7. What are you doing to bring that vision of your legacy to life?

8. How do you feel about that vision of your legacy?

9. Would you like to change what you currently envision as your legacy?

10. If so, what would you like to change – how would you like to be remembered?

YOUR LEADERSHIP STYLE:

1. How would you describe your leadership style?

2. Adaptability: How do you respond to change? Does it take you a while to warm up to a new way of doing things? Or are you an early adopter of new ideas and processes? Does change generally catch you by surprise or can you see it coming from a mile away?

3. Integrity: Can you always been counted on to "Do the Right Thing?" Are you known as a leader who is a straight arrow or one who may occasionally bend the rules? Do you set high standards for yourself, as well as for members of your team?

4. Problem Solving: When addressing a problem at work, do you put more focus on the end result, the Big Picture, or on the individual steps/processes needed to accomplish the ultimate goal?

5. Collaboration: Do you prefer the role of Individual Contributor ("Just tell me when the due date is and I will have it ready for you.") Or Project Team Member ("Let's get everyone together to decide on the direction of the project and brainstorm on solutions to ensure that everyone has an equal say on the path forward.")?

6. Work Style Effectiveness and Efficiency: Are you organized and well-prepared for each workday?

7. Courage: Do you speak on up behalf of others? Do you speak up on behalf of yourself? Would you accept a role leading a team in an area for which you have no expertise?

8. Responsibility and Servant Leadership: Who do you hold accountable when a project fails? How do you do it? Who do you recognize and applaud when a project is successful? How do you do it?

9. Communication: How do you communicate your expectations to your team? How do you ensure that your expectations were communicated clearly?

10. Authenticity and Trust: Are your interactions with your colleagues, peers and team members transparent? Do they trust you? Do you trust them?

CAREER

1. What do you want from your job?

2. What are your key career goals?

3. What skills or knowledge are you developing?

4. How are you investing in your personal and/or professional development?

5. Do your career goals align with your personal life goals? If not, why not?

6. Do you feel valued and appreciated at your current job?

7. What is your level of satisfaction and engagement with your current role?

8. What legacy do you strive to establish and/or maintain? How do you want to be remembered – and for what do you want to be remembered?

9. Are you investing in the professional development of others, creating a pipeline of talented future leaders?

10. What is the best career advice you have ever received or learned on your own?

SELF-ASSESSMENT REVIEW

After completing your Self-Assessment, use these tables to capture your key insights and discoveries:

SELF-ASSESSMENT REVIEW		
Gifts/Talents	Areas of Vulnerability	Values and Beliefs

SELF–ASSESSMENT REVIEW			
Relationships with Others	Destiny/Legacy	Leadership	Career

STRENGTHS – WEAKNESSES – OPPORTUNITIES – THREATS (SWOT)

This tool is a simple, yet highly effective mechanism to visually showcase your Strengths and Weaknesses and identify the Opportunities open to you and the Threats you face.

SWOT Analysis is useful in both business and personal contexts. In business, a SWOT Analysis can assist in various business development strategies, risk assessments, market analysis, etc. In a personal context, it helps you to develop your career in a way that takes best advantage of your talents, abilities and opportunities.

Strengths and Weaknesses are generally <u>internal</u> influences.
Opportunities and Threats generally relate to <u>external</u> factors.

103

Use the questions below to assist in your reflection and analysis.

STRENGTHS:

When thinking about your Strengths, consider them from both an internal perspective (how you see yourself), and from an external point of view (how YOU THINK your colleagues, teammates, peers, customers and others see you):

What advantages do you have?

What do you do better than anyone else?

What do people in your industry see as your strengths?

If you're having difficulty identifying strengths, consider those values and competencies that are respected by your organization; there may be a few of thsse traits that are also strengths of yours.

WEAKNESSES:

As you did with your Strengths, consider your Weaknesses from both an internal perspective (how you see yourself), and from an external point of view (how YOU THINK your colleagues, teammates, peers, customers and others see you):

What could you improve?

What behaviors or habits should you eliminate?

What activities do your colleagues or teammates do at a higher level than you?

What are people in your market likely to see as weaknesses?

Be honest and realistic. Now is the time to face unpleasant truths so that you can begin your journey armed with the insight to make meaningful progress.

OPPORTUNITIES:

What promising opportunities can you identify?

What interesting industry trends are you aware of? How can you leverage those trends to your advantage?

What Strengths can you leverage and transform to Opportunities?

What Weaknesses, if eliminated, can you leverage and transform to Opportunities?

THREATS

What external obstacles do you face?

Are others within your industry faced with the same Threats? What action are they taking to neutralize the Threats?

Are the qualifications for your position changing or likely to change? Are you keeping current with the latest trends/certifications to ensure your ongoing competitiveness for the position you hold/or desire?

Is changing technology or other innovations threatening your position?

Do any of your Weaknesses also represent a Threat to your career advancement?

Bloom Where You Are Planted

Strengths	Weaknesses
What do you do well?	What could you improve?
What unique resources can you draw on?	Where do you have fewer resources than others?
What do others see as your strengths?	What are others likely to see as weaknesses?
Opportunities	**Threats**
What opportunities are open to you?	What threats could harm you?
What trends could you take advantage of?	What is your competition doing?
How can you turn your strengths into opportunities?	What threats do your weaknesses expose you to?

REVIEW YOUR BELIEFS AND VALUES

Now that you have captured key insights from your self-reflection internal assessment and the results of your SWOT analysis, what stands out to you? What did you learn about yourself? What truth did you admit to yourself that you have never given yourself permission to acknowledge? What are your beliefs? What values are important to you? Where do you spend your time and emotional energy?

Do your current beliefs and values align with the outcome you seek? And what can you do to remedy it? What are some of the things you tell yourself that may be preventing you from achieving the outcome you desire? How can you shift those thoughts to create a positive visual image of you achieving the results you seek? How do you plan to implement this transformational change in your thought process?

Use the table below to write down how you envision **being** the change that you want to see. Make note of the **feelings** you need to have that will drive you to do the work you need to do. Then, outline the specific **actions** you need to take in order to achieve the **outcome** you desire.

BE THE CHANGE – DO THE WORK – HAVE THE DESIRED OUTCOME

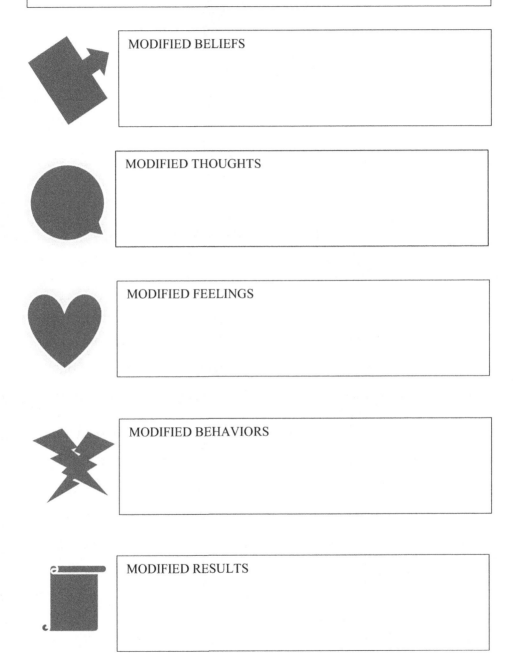

MODIFIED BELIEFS

MODIFIED THOUGHTS

MODIFIED FEELINGS

MODIFIED BEHAVIORS

MODIFIED RESULTS

EXTERNAL ASSESSMENT

360-Degree Feedback Review

A 360-degree feedback review is designed to gather anonymous feedback about an employee from those working most closely with him or her – including direct reports (in the case of managers & supervisors), peers, and managers. In this regard it isn't a typical performance review.

The comments, observations, commendations and constructive criticisms that generally result from a 360-degree feedback review afford you an opportunity to learn things about yourself that you would never have discovered otherwise. You are also able to immediately learn how others view your performance. You can then develop a plan to take action to enhance your strengths and improve upon your areas of vulnerability.

Feedback from a 360-degree review will help you improve your interpersonal interactions, your communication skills, and ultimately, your

110

performance. Your attention will be drawn to any potential blind spots that may exist – without adding undue strain to your relationship. Blind spots, which we will discuss in more detail later, are those differences between how you perceive yourself versus how others perceive you.

If you are seeking transformational change in a professional setting, encourage your employer to support you in receiving a 360-degree review – ask your HR representative or your supervisor to include this commonly used, highly effective tool as a resource for your professional development.

If your request is denied or you are seeking transformational change in a personal capacity, do not hesitate to invest in yourself and hire a professional business coach – a 360-degree review is generally one of the first steps taken as part of the coaching process. However, if you are currently not in a position to retain the services of a professional coach, you can always do it yourself, the old-fashioned way. (See the next section below on Sample External Assessment Feedback Questions for tips).

SAMPLE EXTERNAL ASSESSMENT FEEDBACK QUESTIONS

If you are soliciting external third-party feedback on your own – and not through your company's HR processes or via a professional coaching engagement, feel free to use any of these questions when you request feedback for your External Assessment.

Bloom Where You Are Planted

Select at least 5 – 10 individuals who you feel will provide you with candid feedback. Together, these individuals should represent a 360-degree perspective of your performance. Of this group, individuals should include someone in a higher leadership role and fellow peers and teammates, as well as those at a lower leadership level. It's important that each person has had direct exposure to you and your team and had the opportunity to observe your behaviors and be able to evaluate your performance. Endeavor to make the process as confidential and anonymous as possible.

Allowing participants to submit their feedback through an anonymous channel will lead to more truthful and transparent remarks, both positive and negative. To add more anonymity to the process, you could provide each participant with a self-addressed, stamped envelope by which they could return their responses. You could also ask each person to submit their feedback to another individual who would serve as a third-party intermediary and collect all participants' responses and forward the combined materials to you.

Note: Please be sure to ask each participant to answer the following questions about your job performance. They should emphasize their individual experience working directly with you and your team. It is important for you to learn what people in your organization think you do well in each of these key areas. Likewise, your feedback group should also identify areas for improvement. Encourage each participant to share specific examples to support their remarks.

Leadership

- What are some of the areas of leadership that are of value to your organization?

- Does this employee exhibit leadership qualities in the roles he/she plays in the company?

- If so, can you provide examples of how they positively contribute to the organization through their leadership?

- If not, how can the employee improve their leadership?

Interpersonal Skills

- When this employee works with coworkers, what interpersonal skills do they demonstrate?

- Have you experienced any problems with them interpersonally?

- How would you recommend that the employee improve their interpersonal and relationship-building skills?

Problem Solving

- Does the employee effectively solve problems?

- If so, what are the skills that they have demonstrated in solving problems and arriving at solutions and improvements?

- If less than proficient in problem-solving, in what areas of would you recommend that the employee work to be able to improve their skills?

Motivation

- Does the employee appear to be motivated by his work-related tasks, job, and relationships?

- How does the employee demonstrate that they are motivated and committed to success in the company?

- Have you experienced any difficulties with the level of the employee's motivation?

Efficiency

- Are the employee's work methods and approach to accomplishing their job effective, efficient, and continuously improving?

- Are there areas of improvement that you would recommend for this employee that would help him accomplish their work more effectively?

- Or, are there areas of improvement that would help you accomplish your work more effectively?

PREPARE FOR THE PAIN

Without beating around the bush, I will honestly tell you that receiving candid feedback from your supervisor(s), colleagues and subordinates regarding how you are perceived in the workplace (or other settings), how effective you are (or aren't), and what they consider your strengths and areas of improvement, can be seriously painful – most notably with regard to those areas considered as blind spots. I know this pain from personal experience.

Throughout my professional career, I have been the recipient of 360-degree review feedback four times. It is a tremendously powerful development tool, and one that leaves a lasting imprint. Truthfully, receiving the feedback from a 360-degree review, as helpful as it is, is not for the faint of heart and cannot effectively be absorbed in just one sitting. This is particularly true when you receive this level of in-depth feedback for the first time; because when you see and hear some of the negative and critical feedback, your natural defense mechanisms kick in and you want to discount, justify or just reject the message outright. Or maybe, that was just me.

Be mindful that some of the feedback you will receive through the 360-degree review will be subjective (based on an individual's perceptions, preferences and biases) and some remarks will be more objective (based on observable behaviors or performance data and metrics). Therefore, not all responses should be weighted the same or receive the same amount of focus and energy. The subjective nature of some of the feedback would support the conclusion that reasonable minds might differ on that point. Whereas one participant may describe your leadership style as energetic and authoritative, another may characterize it as aggressive and intimidating. The former invokes executive qualities of charisma and gravitas, the latter sounds like a vicious bully. Which one is right? Maybe both; maybe neither.

It may then be necessary to enlist the help of others; coaches, mentors, sponsors, and/or individuals both within and outside the organization to help you fully evaluate the feedback and determine where to place your focus and devote time and resources to maximize your growth and development. This will lead you to create a definitive growth and development plan, highlighting specific actions you are going to take to better leverage your strengths and minimize your areas of vulnerability.

EXTERNAL ASSESSMENT REVIEW

After reviewing the participants' responses to the External Assessment, use the tables below to capture your key insights and discoveries:

116

EXTERNAL ASSESSMENT REVIEW			
Adaptability	Integrity	Problem Solving	Collaboration

EXTERNAL ASSESSMENT REVIEW			
Courage	Responsibility	Communication	Authenticity and Trust

Compile and Review Results of Internal and External Assessments

Having gone through the self-reflection exercises and solicited feedback from external sources, you are now in a unique and powerful position of personal control. You have within your possession highly valuable and insightful Classified Information. Why do I call it Classified Information? Because it fits the definition to a tee: it is sensitive information that must be protected; access to this information is restricted to only those with a "need to know;" and the mishandling of this information can lead to criminal penalties. (Okay, not that last part – no one is going to jail.)

As such, the proper handling of your Classified Information is a top priority and a matter of national security. (Okay, again, not that last part.) But what you choose to do with this valuable information is an important priority since it has the capacity to directly influence the very transformational changes you are considering. Your Classified Information is a critical component – needed to accelerate your growth and development – to moving you closer to achieving your goals and desired results.

But, we are not finished yet. There are more critical data points we need to add to your collection of Classified Information. Our next action item is to synthesize all the responses, insights, and observations extracted from the results of your Internal and External Assessment Review. Do you observe any common themes amongst the responses? Any outliers? Was any of the feedback new to you? Did it surprise you?

As you review the responses, I invite you to designate the information in the following manner:

CHOOSE ONE

- **Known to Me**
  (you are aware of this information about yourself)

  or

- **Unknown to Me**
  (you were unaware of this information about yourself)

AND

CHOOSE ONE

- **Known About Me by Others** (other people are aware of this information about you)

  or

- **Unknown About Me by Others** (other people were unaware of this information about you)

Information	Known to Me	Unknown to Me	Known About Me by Others	Unknown About Me By Others
Ronetta watches "Saturday Night Live" every weekend	✓		✓	

Once you have designated the information, I invite you to plot it in a simple four-square graph similar to this one:

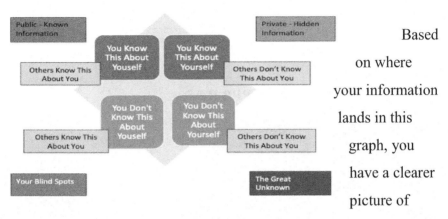

Based on where your information lands in this graph, you have a clearer picture of what information is publicly known about you, what information you hold private, and what information represents a blind spot for you.

From my example then, it is Public – Known Information that I watch "Saturday Night Live" every weekend.

Public - Known Information – Information we know about ourselves that is also known about us by others

Private - Hidden Information – Information we know about ourselves that is NOT known by others

---

Now, let's dig a bit deeper for maximum insight.

From the information designated as Public – Known, Private – Hidden, and Blind Spots, reflect on whether you would consider it either as a Strength or an Area of Vulnerability. Make a note of your reflections here:

PPB Review

	Public - Known Information	Private - Hidden Information	Blind Spots
Strengths			

PPB Review

	Public - Known Information	Private - Hidden Information	Blind Spots
Areas of Vulnerability			

YOU GET TO DECIDE

So, what have you learned so far? Do you have a Blind Spot to one of your Strengths that is widely known by others? Why is that? Is it modesty or humility that prevents you from acknowledging or giving yourself credit for something that others obviously see in you and consider a Strength? Would you like to change that? What impact do you think embracing and better leveraging this Strength would have?

If others see you as a great collaborator, with excellent communication skills and high emotional intelligence – and you have never seen yourself that way (or thought: this feels so natural – nothing out of the ordinary – so why would I get credit for this?), could this be a potential barrier standing in the way of you realizing the outcome you desire? What modifications to your beliefs and thoughts would be required for you to more fully and authentically embrace this Strength? Would you be prepared to commit to internalizing those modifications?

Conversely, do you have a Blind Spot to one of your Areas of Vulnerability? Other folks know you have a vulnerability in a particular area – yet, you are clueless. Why is that? Are you inattentive or are you lacking self-awareness? You just didn't know. Because if you did, you would have already made the necessary changes or at least thought about it. Or, maybe you truly do not value this behavior or skillset; you do not consider it important nor would you allocate any resources (time or money) in that direction.

Going back to our Workaholic example (the relatively anti-social individual who puts in long hours and always delivers above expectations but still can't get promoted): Now you clearly see that others view your lack of interpersonal skills as an Area of Vulnerability; there is less value placed on the number of hours worked or the end product and more value placed on how you make people feel when they work with you. The questions remain: Would you like to make a change in this area? What impact would it have? Are you able to examine your beliefs about the importance of relationships in the workplace? Do you see it as a place to get things done and make money with no time for the soft skills or the chit-chat? Can you even envision yourself asking your colleague on a Monday morning how well their kid performed in the football game the past weekend?

You tell yourself: You have three choices. You can:

1. **Do Nothing:** Stay pigeon-holed in the role you are in, with no chance of promotion because your behaviors do not align with the corporate culture; or

2. **Adapt:** Commit to a development and growth plan that allows you to modify your beliefs and thoughts on the importance of relationships in the workplace, leading you to exhibit authentic behaviors and skills that are valued by your organization; or

3. **Leave:** Find a different organization where your beliefs and behaviors align.

Now is the time to evaluate how you want to proceed. Do the potential transformational changes or modifications align with your core values and beliefs? If so, are you willing to commit to the growth and development process? If not currently aligned, should they be? Are you willing to modify specific beliefs and thoughts to bring about the change you want to see? Or is the potential modification so out of line with your authentic self that you would choose to pass?

You possess all the Classified Information. You have the power. You get to decide.

YOUR INDIVIDUAL GROWTH AND DEVELOPMENT PLAN

Thus far, in the **Bloom Where You Are Planted** framework for transformational change, you have:

o   Cultivated An Attitude of Gratitude

o   Planted Seeds of Positivity

o   Established Firm Roots

     o   Set your intentions – Identified your desired results and outcomes

     o   Assessed your current situation – Compiled Classified Information gained following the examination of your values and beliefs, along with your Strengths and Areas of Vulnerability, through Self-Reflection exercises and feedback from those who know and work with you; considered whether specific modifications to your beliefs and thoughts may be warranted; discovered Known and Hidden Information about you, along with your Blind Spots and their relationship to your Strengths and Areas of Vulnerability

With the completion of these strategic exercises, and the resulting Classified Information within your possession and under your protection, let's move on to crafting your Individual Growth and Development Plan. Feel free to use the sample plan I have attached, or you can create your own – you can even find free development plan templates online.

Whatever development plan format or tool you choose to use, here are a few tips to keep in mind:

1. Identify your development focus

This will be your goal, and the reason for development. You will want to be reminded of what you are working toward and why. It will help keep you motivated throughout the duration of the development process.

2. Identify Strengths and Areas of Vulnerability

Choose 2 – 3 in each area. Decide which Strength(s) you would like to further develop and the Area(s) of Vulnerability you would like to improve, and target those first.

3. Determine the necessary course of action

Consider what existing or anticipated **barriers** may impede either your progress or the final completion of your goal. Think about the **resources** you will need to help you overcome these barriers. Next, detail the specific **action items** that you need to take. Be sure that your identified action items meet the SMART model (Specific, Measurable, Attainable, Relevant and Time-Bound). Be thoughtful as you outline your action plan. Do not rush this process; give yourself ample time to determine the most impactful actions you need to take in order to meet your goals.

4. Include accountability measures

Be sure that you have broken down your goals into highly specific, attainable phases. Include the dates by which each phase is expected to be completed. Set up a recurring meeting with your accountability partner (your supervisor, HR partner, mentor or coach) to ensure you remain on target for completing your goals within the stated timeframe.

5. Improve your plan

Routinely review your plan, and revise, as needed.

Individual Growth and Development Plan					
Identify Area of Focus: **Strength to Leverage** **OR** **Development Opportunity**					
Critical **Behaviors/Activities** Needed to demonstrate skill or competency	**Barriers** Existing or anticipated	**Solutions** Resources needed to overcome Barriers	**Action** **Items** Be SMART	**Target** **Dates**	**Results/Outcomes** What success looks like

Individual Growth and Development Plan					
Identify Area of Focus: **Strength to Leverage** **OR** **Development Opportunity**					
Critical Behaviors/Activities Needed to demonstrate skill or competency	**Barriers** Existing or anticipated	**Solutions** Resources needed to overcome Barriers	**Action Items** Be SMART	**Target Dates**	**Results/Outcomes** What success looks like

Individual Growth and Development Plan					
Identify Area of Focus: **Strength to Leverage** **OR** **Development Opportunity**					
Critical **Behaviors/Activities** Needed to demonstrate skill or competency	**Barriers** Existing or anticipated	**Solutions** Resources needed to overcome Barriers	**Action** **Items** Be SMART	**Target** **Dates**	**Results/Outcomes** What success looks like

"If you can't fly then run, if you can't run then walk, if you can't walk then crawl, but whatever you do, you have to keep moving forward." ~**Martin Luther King, Jr.**

131

BE your authentic self, where your beliefs drive you to DO the actions that lead you to HAVE the results that you desire and align with your core values.

HARD WORK

If it were easy, everyone would do it.

DO THE HARD WORK:

The truth of the matter is, if you want to achieve transformational change, to **Bloom Where You Are Planted**, you cannot get around the fact that you will have to do the work. You cannot expect your desired outcome to magically appear out of thin air without investing the time, resources and emotional energy required. I submit to you that the change in your situation and circumstances will come – but it is waiting on you to be prepared to receive it.

Now is the time to do what you need to do to get the best that will come after. Doing this "inner work" requires you to be open, transparent,

132

authentic, confident and committed. Your transformational change starts on the inside, with a deep examination and challenging of your beliefs, modifying your thoughts, being intentional and more positive about the things you tell yourself about yourself, and the visual images you send to your brain.

During the 2019 MTV Movie and TV Awards, actress Jada Pinkett Smith was honored for being a trailblazer in media. In accepting this award, she acknowledged her own battle with self-doubt, telling herself that she didn't deserve the award. Recognizing the need to silence her Inner Critic, she shared her perspective with the audience. Her impactful and inspirational remarks immediately went viral:

> *"Often, we applaud the trails that people blaze in the external world that we can see.*
>
> *But very rarely do we applaud the trails that are blazed in the hidden rooms of the mind that are full of uncertainty, false beliefs and pain. And it is these internal obstacles that must be challenged in order to muster the courage to forge new paths that we can see in the world.*
>
> *Every last person in this room must do that in some capacity. That means that every last person in this room is a trailblazer, whether within or without."*

The hardest work of the "inner work" is to overcome the uncertainties in our negative self-talk, our insecurities, to become GREAT – who we are intended to be. Everyone has this struggle. There really is no way to get around it. If we want to succeed – to blaze new paths – to be of service at the highest level – to thrive and not just survive, we must do the "inner work" and we have to CONTINUE to do it. Consistency is the key.

I say now: I can do it. You can do it. We can do it.

As you embark upon your "inner work," keep these best practices nearby and refer to them as often as you need:

- Know that you will have good days and bad days; successes and setbacks.

- Expect to feel uncomfortable throughout this process. My advice: get comfortable being uncomfortable.

- Be patient. Transformational change is an ongoing process that just simply takes time to achieve. There are no shortcuts.

- Be intentionally present and engaged. You are doing amazing things and you should experience it all. Don't "phone it in" or try to hurry it along.

- Keep your eyes on the prize and don't give up.

- Honor your emotions – whether you are feeling happy or sad, angry or excited, frustrated or motivated – be present in that moment; try not to diminish, hide or push any of your emotions away.

- Practice self-care. Get plenty of rest. Exercise. Eat well. Take a walk. Ride your bike. Go to the movies. Soak in the tub. Do these things because they make you feel better, not because it's another "to-do" agenda item.

- Be bold. Take risks. Do not be ruled by fear. Most folks aren't actually afraid to take a risk or to fail; they are afraid of letting other people see them fail. What other people think about you and what you're doing is more about them than you.

- Mind your business. While doing your "inner work," pursuing your passion, learning a new skill or just daring to live your best life in the most authentic way possible, what other people think is none of your business and should not concern you. Mind Your Business.

One day? Or Day One. You decide.

DIGGING DEEPER
ESTABLISH FIRM ROOTS

Defining Your Short-Term Career Goals

Consider what you would like to achieve for your career within the next 12 - 24 months.

What are your Short-Term Career Goals?

In what Industry or Area of Interest do you envision working?

What Position or Job Title (level of responsibility) do you envision holding?

Do you already possess the necessary skills, competencies, licenses/certifications or knowledge to work in that Industry or your Area of Interest?

If not, list the specific areas where you need to dig deep and develop the skills, competencies, licenses/certifications or knowledge required for the Industry or Area of Interest.

Do you already possess the necessary skills, competencies, licenses/certifications or knowledge to hold that Position or Job Title?

If not, list the specific areas where you need to dig deep and develop the skills, competencies, licenses/certifications or knowledge required for the Position or Job Title.

SHORT-TERM GOALS		
Industry/Position	Areas for Development	Plans for Development

Long-Term Career Goals:

Consider what you would like to achieve for your career within the next 3 – 5 years.

What are your Long-Term Career Goals?

In what Industry or Area of Interest do you envision working?

What Position or Job Title (level of responsibility) do you envision holding?

Do you already possess the necessary skills, competencies, licenses/certifications or knowledge to work in that Industry or your Area of Interest?

If not, list the specific areas where you need to dig deep and develop the skills, competencies, licenses/certifications or knowledge required for the Industry or Area of Interest.

Do you already possess the necessary skills, competencies, licenses/certifications or knowledge to hold that Position or Job Title?

If not, list the specific areas where you need to dig deep and develop the skills, competencies, licenses/certifications or knowledge required for the Position or Job Title.

LONG-TERM GOALS		
Industry/Position	Areas for Development	Plans for Development

Chapter 6: EMBRACE GROWTH

AS LEAVES AND FLOWER BUDS EMERGE
Develop Effective and Successful Relationships with Mentors, Coaches and Sponsors

A lot of people have gone further than they thought they could because someone else thought they could.

MENTORS, COACHES, & SPONSORS –
POWEERFUL RELATIONSHIPS TO SUPPORT AND ADVANCE YOUR GROWTH

Just as your journey to ***Bloom Where You Are Planted*** firmly takes root, you will begin to notice an internal shift resulting from your intentional focus and dedication to the "inner work" you have been doing. A shift in what you believe about yourself, what you tell yourself about yourself, as well as how you feel and how you act. Externally, your commitment to this developmental process will also be unmistakable; your inclusion and utilization of Mentors, Coaches and Sponsors will sprout evidence of your continued growth as they not only actively participate

141

and propel you in your journey – they are personally invested in your success.

The role that each of these individuals plays in supporting your personal and/or professional growth and development and advancement of your career may differ; however, ultimately each role is vitally important and each individual serving in such a capacity is deeply committed to seeing you progress and succeed.

How important is it to have such support? I submit to you: Ms. Oprah Winfrey. Because of her commitment to promoting talent and to sharing with her vast network the individuals, services and products that she appreciates and values, she has breathed life into new upstarts, made celebrities out of regular folks and created multi-millionaires. Due to Ms. Winfrey's far-reaching influence, support and advocacy, she has launched the careers of the following professionals and service-providers to a completely different stratosphere:

- Dr. Phil (retired psychologist with his own television show since 2002, earning more than $15M/year);
- Dr. Oz (practicing physician with his own television show);
- Suze Orman (financial advisor whose prior television show now generates more than $10M in earnings, due to Orman's numerous appearances on The Oprah Winfrey Show "TOWS");

- Rachael Ray (cooking show skyrocketed and led to multiple other successful ventures due to her numerous appearances on TOWS);
- there's also her trainer Bob Greene;
- interior designer Nate Berkus;
- lifestyle coach and minister Iyanla Vanzant;
- BFF Gayle King, and any author highlighted in Oprah's Book Club.

And there are more – so many more who owe their careers and livelihood to Ms. Oprah Winfrey. While these are truly extreme examples, because there are only a small handful of individuals with the same level of access, exposure and influence as this country's first African American female self-made billionaire, the underlying principles and the value of these supportive relationships remain the same.

So, let's spend a little time exploring each of these relationships, the role they serve, the value you can expect to receive from each, how to find them and how to nurture them.

Briefly, a **mentor** is someone who typically works in the same company as the mentee, and the mentoring relationship is generally focused on providing sound, actionable advice. A **coach** is usually an external resource who plays a hand in helping their clients grow and develop on both a personal and professional level in a relatively short period of time, generally within a three- to six-month period. A **sponsor** is most often a senior-level leader employed at the same organization who is personally involved and deeply invested in the further development and success of the sponsored employee.

A Mentor talks with you, a Coach talks to you, and a Sponsor talks about you.

WHO ARE THEY – WHAT DO THEY DO?

Mentors

Mentors can guide you, help you, take you under his or her wing, and nurture your career aspirations. They usually have greater years of experience in a particular field and provide guidance to an individual with less experience to increase their potential for success in their career goals. Here, meeting the career needs of the mentee is important to this development-driven, relationship-oriented process.

Mentors can help you assess your strengths and weaknesses, foster a sense of belonging within the organization, and help you navigate the company culture and politics, as well as let you know who the organization's key players are. Mentors can also be leveraged to assist in working through career and workplace issues; they can provide a fresh

144

perspective – a new set of eyes – and assist in brainstorming ideas for a strategy to resolve and overcome challenges.

Coaches

Coaches allow their clients to grow by discovering and defining their personal and career goals, creating a plan for achieving those goals, and receiving consistent feedback and guidance, which helps the client acquire new skills and improve overall performance and engagement. Coaches may also be leveraged to work through workplace challenges.

Coaching is a task-oriented, performance-driven relationship that is tailored to the specific needs of their client. Coaches may incorporate such data as the client's performance history, past experiences, and 360-degree feedback from the client's manager(s), peers and other third parties familiar with the client.

Coaching clients generally report that the relationship positively impacted their careers as well as their lives by helping them to:

- Establish and take action towards achieving goals
- Improve their individual performance
- Become more self-reliant
- Gain more job and life satisfaction
- Contribute more effectively to the team and the organization
- Take greater responsibility and accountability for actions and commitments
- Communicate more effectively

While coaching relationships may begin for a variety of reasons (from both the employee and the organization), when considering a coaching relationship, keep in mind that coaching is not intended as a disciplinary action or a training session, and should never be used as a substitute for therapy.

Sponsors

Sponsors are senior leaders with status and influence who strongly believe in the potential of an individual and will therefore advocate for them, opening doors to enable their next big career move. Personal investment by the sponsor could lead to them developing successful strategies to ensure the sponsored employee has the needed education, experience and exposure required for a promotion or raise. Because it requires a senior executive to spend his or her own political capital and put his or her own credibility on the line to give an underling a leg up, entering into a sponsorship relationship is far riskier than engaging in a mentoring role.

To equalize the employment playing field, access to effective and committed sponsor relationships is critically important for people of color and women in the workplace because white males are still more likely to obtain powerful sponsors than underrepresented members of the organization. Studies have further shown that even "high-potential" women in the workforce are over-mentored and under-sponsored when compared to their male counterparts. This lack of sponsorship leads to fewer women being appointed to high-visibility roles in the organization and fewer women who will consider putting their hat in the ring to compete for those top jobs.

A few examples of the benefits from partnering with an engaged and effective sponsor would include when that sponsor:

- Hires you for a position that allows you to learn a different segment of the business and increase your ability to advance even further;
- Actively considers and seeks out openings, assignments, and opportunities that will enhance your exposure among other senior leaders, also increasing your ability to advance;
- Connects personally and directly with decision makers who have the authority to say "yes" to an opportunity or promotion for you;
- Speaks up for your skills and supports your candidacy when your name or potential opportunities come up; or
- Tells you what steps to take and what you need to know to improve your chances of being selected for the opening or opportunity.

HOW DO YOU FIND THEM?

Mentors

When searching for a Mentor, consider whether your current employer, your college alma mater, or other organizations with which you're already associated have a formal mentoring program in place. In these structured arrangements, participants may be given personality assessments so that "mentees" can be matched with compatible mentors. Other organizations have found that when mentors and mentees are very different, greater opportunities for discovery emerge.

To find a mentor on your own, identify someone you admire and respect. You can choose someone from your place of employment or outside the organization – or both; having more than one mentor is not only accepted, it is expected since each mentor has a defined area of expertise that you may be able to leverage to advance your career.

Coaches

When considering a coaching engagement, your company may either provide direct access to an executive and/or career coach or may provide you with a list of coaching professionals who have either previously worked with or are sanctioned by the organization. If you prefer to keep your desire to use a career coach a bit more discrete, there are a plethora of online resources to guide you in your search for a coach.

During your first consultation with a potential coach before engaging their services (which I highly recommend), think of it as an interview process during which you are expected to select the most qualified professional, with whom you have a rapport, and who you feel can help you reach your development goals and objectives in a manner that closely aligns with your authentic values and beliefs. During the interview, consider asking questions about the following:

1. How the coach handles confidentiality;
2. Whom do they consider as their client – you or the company (this is a critical question especially if the company is paying the cost for the coaching engagement);
3. The extent of their coaching experience and success rate with leaders who have a similar background as you;
4. Their coaching philosophy and processes.

Sponsors

You don't find sponsors – they find you.

To increase your likelihood of attracting a sponsor who can help you find opportunities to learn and grow in your career, you have to show that you're worth that risk and effort. You should seek out and volunteer for opportunities that will allow you to interact with those who are in more senior positions than you, and also have clout and power. Get involved in networking and professional groups that include professionals in higher-level roles both in your organization or in related organizations.

Most importantly, though, attracting a potential sponsor means you must have an extraordinary success record (history), and have demonstrated your potential to continue this record of success at the next level and beyond (future).

IDEAL CHARACTERISTICS

Mentors

In an effective and successful mentoring relationship, mentors will encourage your goals, provide honest and constructive feedback, help you develop self-awareness, challenge you to grow beyond your perceived limitations, introduce you to movers and shakers, motivate you to join professional organizations that can help you advance, and above all, listen to you and be easy to communicate with.

Underrepresented members in the workforce, including women and people of color, may find it helpful to seek out mentors/role models of the same background so they can identify with the success of someone who has made it in a diverse workforce. However, do not fall into the misperception that, as a woman or person of color, your mentors, coaches or sponsors need to look like you in order for the relationship to work to your benefit. You could be excluding, overlooking or completely disregarding the very person who has the ability, interest, capacity and influence to help you meet your career goals and/or take your goals to the next level.

Decide what you need in a mentor and what skills you'd like to develop with your mentor's support. Consider your goals in choosing a mentor. Remember: you can have more than one mentor.

Resist asking your direct supervisor to be your mentor; your relationship should be open and transparent enough that you feel free to share concerns you may have about your career and other workplace issues, and you are not likely to have that level of comfort with a direct supervisor as a mentor.

Coaches

The foundation of a positive, strong coaching relationship is trust. An employee needs to believe that there is a high level of confidentiality regarding information that is discussed and trust that their coach will be discreet when assisting with their development. Coaches should convey a level of confidence that enables the coaching process to proceed quickly, focusing on the coaching goals rather than on irrelevant matters. Coaches who are good listeners and provide accountability – holding clients to their performance goals – increase the likelihood of establishing the right tone with their clients to ensure that their concerns and needs are heard and that desired goals are being met. An ideal coach will also recognize and assist their client in eliminating self-limiting beliefs and counter-productive behaviors and is an excellent cheerleader in celebrating their clients' successes.

Sponsors

Sponsors should know you and your work very well to ensure that you continue to be successful in any subsequent positions. Sponsors should proactively seek out opportunities that may interest you and advocate on your behalf in addition to the sponsor being willing to use their influence to promote your success.

PERSONAL AGREEMENTS SUPPORTING YOUR NEW GROWTH

Several years ago, I discovered a little book that had a big message. In, *"The Four Agreements,"* by Don Miguel Ruiz, the author explores the power of self-limiting beliefs and how these beliefs rob us of our joy and create needless pain and suffering. He provides a path towards self-love and peace.

Living a life of joy, in full-bloom, requires us to summon the strength, confidence and courage to deeply examine and then modify or completely release those fear-based beliefs that lead us to experience needless pain and suffering and cause us to fail and hold us back.

Challenge yourself to honor these four simple, yet life-enriching, powerful agreements in your relationships with your mentor, sponsors and coaches (everyone, really) – and with yourself to authentically embrace your power and to flourish magnificently in your brilliance: (1) Be impeccable with your word; (2) Don't take anything personally; (3) Don't make assumptions; and (4) Always do your best.

I told you they were simple, right? Now, let's explore their power.

Be impeccable with your word.

- Be truthful: Say what you mean and mean what you say.
- Honor your commitments: Do what you say you will do.
- Know that your words have power. Recall that the power of "I am" confirms: You are what and what you say you are. And conversely, the same is also true: You are not who and what you say you are not.
- Transform your negative talk about yourself – and others.
- Speak Life. Speak Health. Speak Prosperity. Speak Love.

Don't take anything personally.

- The behavior and attitude of others is MORE a reflection of who THEY are – THEIR beliefs and experiences and THEIR fears and insecurities – and has LITTLE to do with you.
- This is a hard one to grasp because things happen TO us; people are mean TO us; rude/disrespectful/untruthful TO us.

Mastering this agreement will take intentional effort and continued practice. The goal here is step out of the cycle of tying your self-worth, self-esteem or identity to the words and behaviors of others. This concept can present a challenge to master as many of us have been indoctrinated or conditioned from a very early age to find our worth in the opinions and behaviors of others. We were told to be nice, to serve and please others, and we were rewarded for doing so. Breaking that cycle will require tremendous "inner work" to determine whether holding on to such beliefs serve us or rather do us harm.

Don't make assumptions.

- ASSUME = ASS + U + ME
- If something is not clear to you – ask. Seek clarity
- Communicate to avoid misunderstandings.

In today's technology-driven world, where children are born knowing how to use a smartphone (they are taking selfies in the delivery room now, aren't they?), what I am about to share is radical and unheard of. For the clearest communications, do not text/email/DM/Snapchat when you can pick up the telephone and have a conversation. Next, when you can (and here's the really radical part), put down the phone and have a personal conversation – especially when the person you need to communicate with is in the next room or down the hall or just an elevator ride away.

Always do your best.

- YOUR best comes from the amount of energy, commitment, time, etc. you have available

❧ YOUR best will vary depending on your situation, health, other obligations, etc.

❧ If you know you have given YOUR very best – and not an excuse you have given yourself for shirking responsibility or not living up to the fullest potential for which you yourself know you are capable – this knowledge will help to free you from an abundance of self-doubt and other self-limiting behaviors.

By honoring these four powerful agreements, you are harnessing and strengthening your personal power; the resulting increased sense of strength and confidence will empower you to break the hold that fear-based beliefs have and accelerate your growth as you Bloom.

DIGGING DEEPER

EMBRACE GROWTH AS LEAVES AND FLOWER BUDS EMERGE

Develop Effective and Successful Relationships with Mentors, Coaches and Sponsors

To fully support your progress thus far and to aid in future personal and professional development, consider how you can attract and secure engaged and committed mentors, coaches and sponsors.

- Do you currently have individuals who you can identify as a Mentor, a Coach and a Sponsor? Yes, you need all three.

- If yes, evaluate the effectiveness and success of each relationship.

- Are you receiving the expected benefits? Are you doing your part to nurture that relationship and make it a win-win proposition (for mentors and sponsors, only)?

- If you cannot identify an existing relationship with a Mentor, Coach and Sponsor, explore why you haven't established these relationships.

- What are the barriers? What resources are needed to overcome these barriers?

- What actions are needed to increase your likelihood of attracting and securing the Mentors, Coaches and Sponsors that best align with your values and desired career goals?

156

Chapter 7: **ENJOY YOUR FULL BLOOM**
Celebrate Your Successes

Celebrate every success, no matter how small the win, to cultivate a mindset of success.

YOU DID IT. CELEBRATE IT!

Often, we get caught up in the process of change, so caught up in our circumstances, that as we go through this developmental process, we forget to appreciate the work, the change, the growth that we have accomplished. We undervalue it, we devalue it, and we lose sight of the progress that we're actually making. Let me ask you: Was yesterday a good day? Did you finish a tough project, learn something new or complete a small but important step toward achieving a much bigger goal? What did you do to recognize those achievements? Anything? Little victory dance? Or did you simply move on to the next task, project or assignment without giving your success another thought? I get it: we have so many agenda items on our To-Do list – we have to just keep pushing forward, right? After all, successfully completing that task or project is its own reward; and it is important to stay humble.

Well, as it turns out, by giving permission to feel joy and satisfaction and to acknowledge the measure of dedication and courage – no matter how small – it took to achieve a goal actually increases positive emotions such as self-respect, happiness, and confidence. This is excellent news for anyone on a journey of transformational change – to *Bloom Where You Are Planted.*

What is the rationale of celebrating incremental successes when there is still an overwhelmingly large list of items to do – goals to accomplish? The fact is that by not recognizing, or downplaying, our successes, we are telling ourselves that we haven't done enough to celebrate or that we don't deserve the recognition or the celebration. And we already know the effects of such powerful negative thoughts. Personally, I know this mindset and these thoughts all too well. I had always prided myself as being a "Big Picture" individual; only easing up or slowing down once the entire endeavor was completed. Then, unfortunately after the sudden and unexpected loss of a friend, I re-evaluated many of my belief systems and concluded that to delay acknowledging or celebrating incremental successes served no real purpose. Being faced with the fragility of life reinforced the necessity of not putting off doing something positive to another day – that really isn't promised to us anyway. I gave myself permission to feel joy, and I

158

embraced this new mindset with gusto. Not one to generally make a big production of my birthday – the year I turned 50, I celebrated. *All. Year. Long.* It was entertaining to explain to my daughter why the purchase of a handbag in March was "for my birthday," when she was fully aware that birthday wasn't until August.

What are you holding yourself back from celebrating? Don't worry. It doesn't have to be a huge, grand affair. It's not the size of the celebration that counts – what is important is acknowledging that you are growing and creating your best life. And when you notice and celebrate your successes, you start to see yourself as someone who is successful rather than someone who's trying to become successful.

There's another reason to stop and smell the roses; to pause and reflect on our journey and what we have accomplished along the way. Quite simply: it makes us feel good. When we celebrate, our brains release endorphins, chemicals that create feelings of euphoria and well-being. So, when we accomplish something and don't take the time to celebrate, we are robbing ourselves of an important feeling that reinforces our success. Quite frankly, that sounds counterproductive to our goals for pursuing transformational change. Why would we do that?

On top of that, when we fail to celebrate our many accomplishments, we are training our brains that what we are doing isn't all that exciting and important. If every day feels mundane (even when we are crushing it) we will stop giving 110% and end up with less than stellar results. We end up feeling empty, lacking focus and performing poorly. And, why would we do that?

So, it's settled. In order to fully embrace the growth that we have realized through the midst of our challenges – to Bloom Where We Have Been Planted – we have to celebrate each success along the journey. We have to; it's science. And you can't argue with science.

So, Celebrate You.

Today.

You Deserve It.

You Did It!

Congratulations!!

DIGGING DEEPER

ENJOY YOUR FULL BLOOM

Celebrate Your Successes

How will you celebrate your successes?

The size of the celebration/recognition is not important. Big or Small – Just stop for a moment to honor your achievement and say to yourself: **"Yes!! I did it!"**

What speaks to you and makes you feel special?

*A massage or mani-pedi

*A facial

*A night out with friends

*A quiet night in

*Going to the movies

*Going to the bookstore

*Retail therapy

*A visit to the museum

*Dinner at your favorite restaurant

*Fresh flowers

*Taking a vacation

*A cupcake – or 2

*Adding to your collection of thimbles, figurines, dolls, handbags . . .

FROM ME TO YOU

As our time together draws to a close, I sincerely thank you for the time and energy you invested during this journey. My prayer is that as you explored each of the transformational change strategies, you felt a bit more empowered, a bit more sure of yourself, a bit more fired up to do the "inner work" for your personal growth and development – especially if the mere thought of you facing the negative, self-limiting beliefs that your Inner Critic has etched deep within your being makes you break out into a cold sweat. Be assured: your Inner Critic does not have the final say – you do.

To support you everyI leave you with these final thoughts:

❀ Make every effort to be kind to yourself. Be intentional and allow yourself the grace that you would freely give others. Recognize and appreciate that this process takes time, and while you may see and feel some changes almost immediately, a complete transformation of your belief systems, thoughts and actions take time – so give yourself a break.

❀ Document your journey. We all have a unique and powerful story to share. Every step of your transformational journey to **Bloom Where You Are Planted** is meaningful and an integral part of the entire process. Use your journal to capture your daily thoughts, insights, feelings, victories and setbacks. You will have a much deeper appreciation for your all that you have accomplished when you are able to review the peaks and valleys along the way. Also, an extraordinarily phenomenal connection between the aspirational and the achieved occurs when you actually commit your goals, dreams and desires to writing.

Bring along an accountability partner. By letting someone else know of your intentions for transformational change increases the likelihood of your success tremendously. We tend to work harder, and hold truer to our commitments when there is someone who will lovingly support our efforts, hold us accountable and keep us focused on our goals.

Have fun. Enjoy the journey. Find something to celebrate – even on those day when celebrating feels like the absolute last thing you want to do. Seek out the silver lining – and share it with others. Put the challenges you are facing in perspective by volunteering to help someone . Give of yourself for the benefit of someone else.

Claim your victory. You've got this all under control. Embrace the fact that your change already exists within you – that you currently possess everything you need to Bloom Where You Are Planted.